New Approaches Towards the 'Good Life'

Hans-Uwe Otto
Sabine Schäfer (eds.)

New Approaches Towards the 'Good Life'

Applications and Transformations of the Capability Approach

Barbara Budrich Publishers
Opladen • Berlin • Toronto 2014

All rights reserved. No part of this publication may be reproduced, stored in or introduced into a retrieval system, or transmitted, in any form, or by any means (electronic, mechanical, photocopying, recording or otherwise) without the prior written permission of Barbara Budrich Publishers. Any person who does any unauthorized act in relation to this publication may be liable to criminal prosecution and civil claims for damages.

You must not circulate this book in any other binding or cover and you must impose this same condition on any acquirer.

A CIP catalogue record for this book is available from
Die Deutsche Bibliothek (The German Library)

© 2014 by Barbara Budrich Publishers, Opladen, Berlin & Toronto
www.barbara-budrich.net

ISBN 978-3-8474-0157-5
eISBN 978-3-8474-0466-8

Das Werk einschließlich aller seiner Teile ist urheberrechtlich geschützt. Jede Verwertung außerhalb der engen Grenzen des Urheberrechtsgesetzes ist ohne Zustimmung des Verlages unzulässig und strafbar. Das gilt insbesondere für Vervielfältigungen, Übersetzungen, Mikroverfilmungen und die Einspeicherung und Verarbeitung in elektronischen Systemen.

Die Deutsche Bibliothek – CIP-Einheitsaufnahme
Ein Titeldatensatz für die Publikation ist bei der Deutschen Bibliothek erhältlich.
Verlag Barbara Budrich Barbara Budrich Publishers
Stauffenbergstr. 7. D-51379 Leverkusen Opladen, Germany

86 Delma Drive. Toronto, ON M8W 4P6 Canada
www.barbara-budrich.net

Jacket illustration by Bettina Lehfeldt, Kleinmachnow –
www.lehfeldtgraphic.de
Printed in Europe on acid-free paper by paper&tinta, Warsaw
Editing by Alison Romer, Lancaster, UK
Typographical Editing by Ulrike Weingärtner, Gründau, Germany

Content

Sabine Schäfer & Hans-Uwe Otto
Introduction: A Social Sciences Perspective on the
Capability Approach ... 7

Conceptual Inquiries Into the Capability Approach

Rada Jancic
Intersubjectivity and Recognition in Serbian Primary Schools:
The Contribution of Paul Ricœur to the Capability Approach ... 17

Erika Bozzato
The Contribution of Critical Discourse Analysis to the Capability
Approach in Education Policy Analysis: The Case of Kosovo ... 33

Anika Duveneck
The Contribution of Critical Materialist Theory to Capability
Research: Empirical Insights From the Field of Local Educational
Politics ... 53

Education and the Capability Approach

Joshua Eshuchi
Human Capital, Capabilities and Education Quality in Kenya ... 73

Antoanneta Potsi
Greek Pre-primary Teachers' Beliefs and Practices: Are they
Capabilities- or Performance-based? ... 89

Lakshmi N. Venkataraman
Caste, Class and Education: Intersectional Implications of
Capability Formation in a South Indian Village ... 107

Capabilities of Young People

Franziska Eisenhuth
Refugee Children in Germany: Acting Within a Framework
of Capability Constraints   125

Bettina Ritter
Capabilities of Young Mothers in Welfare Institutions: What Can
the Capability Approach Learn From Biographical Research?   141

Natalia Karmaeva
Reframing Teaching: A New Chance of Agency for Teaching
Academics in Germany   159

Index   175

Sabine Schäfer & Hans-Uwe Otto

Introduction: A Social Sciences Perspective on the Capability Approach

The Capability Approach (CA) is a normative and justice-based framework for conceptualizing and evaluating people's well-being or, in other words, for supporting the development of public policies that provide people with plural options to be and to do what they have reason to value. Depending on which version of the approach a researcher follows, the focus lies either on providing the informational base for judging justice in a society (Amartya Sen) or on debates about the human good (Martha Nussbaum). However, the CA delivers neither a theory of the social world nor a methodology to research it. It needs to be combined with explanatory concepts and methods that have the potential to bring to light the conditions, requirements, assumptions, and the like that shape people's ideas about their options for different ways of life (see Robeyns 2005: 94). In other words, the CA serves as the fertile base for producing new approaches towards the analysis and facilitation of the 'good life' of persons, in case it is complemented by other concepts. The social sciences deliver such concepts and are thus appropriate candidates for linking the empirical realities of the social world to the normative stance of social justice given by the CA (see Zimmermann 2006).

The chapters in this volume bring together numerous experiences in establishing such links between the social sciences and the CA gained at the Research School Education and Capabilities (Educap), an international graduate school at the German universities of Bielefeld and Dortmund founded in 2008. About 40 doctoral researchers from all over the world have been or are still working on their empirical PhD projects at Educap. The School's thematic focus is on the broad research field of education, including not only institutions of the educational system (such as pre-schools, schools, or universities), families, and the labour market but also social policies and the living conditions of children and young people in general.[1] The dissertations produced in the context of Educap constitute a substantial step forward in the development of conceptual connections between the CA and the theories and methodologies of the social sciences.

---

1   Educap was funded from 2008 to 2013 by the Ministry of Innovation, Science, and Technology of the German federal state of North Rhine-Westphalia and the two participating universities. For more information about Educap, see http://www.educap.tu-dortmund.de/cms/en/home/

The research strategies pursued by the contributors to this volume have been both challenging and fruitful. Applying CA concepts to empirical research questions addressing, for example, the deprivation of young mothers or refugee children in Germany or the subjective theories and practices of teachers in Serbia or Greece is a challenging venture, because these questions need a strong foundation in social science theories and methodologies. Therefore, the CA concepts had to be thought through and adapted to these new fields of research. We believe that the CA can benefit from this work, because an analysis informed by the concepts and methodologies of the social sciences allows us to reconstruct the social contexts and conditions in which the option spaces for action, and thus for the development of capabilities, actually emerge. On the other hand, the work has been worthwhile and fruitful for the social science perspective as well, because the strong orientation towards agency inherent in the CA opens up a view on the agents' resources rather than their deficits – the latter being found more commonly in the research field of social inequalities in the social sciences. Thus, to make the CA applicable for research in the social sciences, it may be justified to conceptualize it from the perspective of action theory. Furthermore, the CA is oriented towards changing existing societal conditions to achieve more social justice. This orientation is still missing in the major part of the social sciences, especially sociology, which focuses almost completely on analysis rather than engaging in critique and becoming actively committed to social change (see Sayer 2008).

When we talk about the 'Capability Approach' in this volume, we include both main versions, that of Amartya Sen and that of Martha Nussbaum. Most of the studies collected in this volume build upon the writings of both authors and their respective followers, because this offers the best way to implement the CA in an empirical social sciences study. Whereas Sen's version provides an architecture of the CA that allows us to analyse the issue of the freedom of real persons in much greater detail (Sen 1999), Nussbaum's list of ten basic human capabilities (Nussbaum 2007) offers a metric for assessing not only social policies and politics but also people's concrete living situations. Thus, which version is applied depends predominantly on the research focus of the particular study. In other words, we do not intervene in the philosophical debates about which version is more convincing or justifiable, but simply use both versions in what is more of an instrumental way in order to enrich empirical research projects embedded in the social sciences – especially education science and sociology.

The CA does not just draw the researcher's attention to what individuals actually do, their functionings, as is mostly the case in current education and social research. With the concept of capabilities, it also offers a frame for analysing the options for action that persons recognize for the formation of what they themselves perceive as a 'good life'. Following the French sociologist Pierre Bourdieu, we can call the concept of capabilities a thinking tool designed not to sort the social world into prefixed categories but to satisfy the relational character of the social world in which the impact of practices depends on the social context in which they occur (see Bourdieu/Wacquant 1992). The capabilities thinking tool contains the idea that a person should have plural alternatives for action at her disposal, and that she is able to choose freely between them. Thus, we could say that the autonomous person first has the ability to inspect all the different options and then choose one that serves her own life plan best; and, second, the ability to put that choice into practice as a functioning.

This means that the concept of capabilities contains demanding presuppositions that make its implementation into social science research a major challenge for the two core categories of the social sciences: the individual and society. The individual, on the one hand, is conceptualized in the context of the CA as a person who already has certain characteristics at her disposal, especially a high degree of critical reflection that allows her to develop a life plan, to recognize options for action, and to reconcile one with the other. In doing so, it is necessary to neutralize so-called 'adaptive preferences' – preferences that do not originate from reflection but, for example, from adaptation to cultural or religious traditions or economic conditions (see Khader 2011). However, it is not quite clear where the person as a socialized individual has gained these characteristics, because the CA has yet to conceptualize the process of socialization. Society, on the other hand, appears only faintly in the CA. Whereas Sen leaves the concept of society completely open, simply stressing the importance of deliberative political processes, Nussbaum is interested in individuals on the one hand and policies of the national state on the other. This national state has to provide structures that first make opportunity freedom possible, such as institutions and opportunities for participation oriented towards ideals of social justice. Again, it does not become clear how the relation between the national state and its institutions is conceptualized in the frame of the CA (see Otto/Ziegler 2013). However, in the social sciences, the term society includes all the relations between individuals and other social actors such as institutions and organizations. Moreover, the CA does not clarify the relation between society and the individual, the central research focus of the social sciences. This makes it hard to detect where exactly the individual is situated in the architecture of the CA, not to mention where institutions are situated.

Because the CA has been designed as a philosophical approach to a theory of justice, it does not need to take all these conceptual problems into account. But some of these problems also emerge in the debates among the proponents of the CA. For example, how to apply the CA to individuals who do not dispose of the necessary critical reflection such as children or the mentally disabled remains an open question (see Nussbaum 2007). Thus, the

CA is scarcely spelled out for areas such as education or socialization. This does not mean that the importance of social context for action is neglected in general. It gets 'a room of its own' in the concept of conversion factors, factors that are perceived to be decisive for the transformation of resources into capabilities (see Robeyns 2011), even though this room is only small and it is not quite clear where it is located.

Initially, the CA was developed from the perspectives of political economics and political philosophy. Thus, it is no surprise that social science concepts do not appear at its centre. Up to now, one principal field of its application has been in development studies and politics. However, some social and education researchers have begun to apply the term human development to educational processes more generally in the context of several empirical research projects.[2] They are thereby beginning to orient the CA more towards the social sciences and, with regard to the conceptualization of the person, towards a continental European philosophy that stresses the individual's membership of social groups more than is usually the case in Anglo-Saxon research traditions. In philosophy, Paul Ricœur (2005) with his concept of '*l'homme capable*' has even developed his own version of a capability approach that concentrates on the individual's recognition by the social group from the perspective of philosophy of language. Thus, he follows a direction related to the concepts of 'me' and 'self' developed by George Herbert Mead in the context of his symbolic interaction theory that also built upon the interaction of the individual with others. This could be a gateway for socialization research into the CA that has yet to be really opened up.

The problems that arise when applying the CA to empirical research are mostly regarded as a matter of operationalization. The conceptual challenges that originate from the lack of concepts applicable to social science research in the CA, such as a concept of society, the localization of the individual or institutions, or the role of the social context, have yet to be discussed in depth. The need for conceptual work on such concepts in the context of the CA evolved during the research processes of the studies conducted at Educap. However, all the chapters in this volume demonstrate that it is well worth facing this challenge in order to benefit from the idea of social change that is inherent to the CA but often missing in social science research.

The volume is structured in three sections. The first section focuses on conceptual blind spots in the CA such as the relation between individual and community, the role of the social context and power relations in the structure of the CA, and the consideration of the political-economic logics of capitalism. The second section addresses the implementation of capabilities-

---

[2] As well as single projects running throughout the world, there have been several Collaborative Projects funded by the European Union in recent years that build on the CA in the context of social policy, social and education science, and related subjects (e.g. CAPRIGHT, WorkAble, and SocIEtY).

oriented thinking to education systems and the practice of actors. The topic of the third section is the operationalization of capabilities in the context of qualitative studies on young people in different living situations in Germany.

The first section begins with the chapter by *Rada Jancic* who analyses how far Serbian primary school teachers are aware of their professional task to support the development of capabilities in their pupils. She adds the capabilities version of the French philosopher Paul Ricœur to the CA and uses his core concept of 'recognition' to show how the development of capabilities is determined to a certain extent by the community group. She suggests conceptualizing recognition as a social conversion factor in the frame of the CA. In her study on education policy in Kosovo, *Erika Bozzato* also focuses on the role of the social context in the CA. Her analysis unveils how social context and power relations remain 'black boxes' in the CA, even though it aims to evaluate public policies based on these dimensions. She suggests adding Critical Discourse Analysis to the CA, because it provides methodologies that cast light on the conditions of social context and power relations in policy analysis combined with a critical stance towards society. *Anika Duveneck* takes a different critical stance in the third chapter of this section. By combining the CA with Critical Materialist Theory in her analysis of German local educational politics, she shows how the logics of capitalist societies shape public policies as well as the lives of people. She is able to overcome a common deficiency of policy analysis: by ignoring how political economic processes impact on actors and social reality in general, it often draws partial and misleading conclusions.

The second section starts with a chapter that confronts two different programmes in Kenyan education policy. *Joshua Eshuchi* argues that education quality has to be assessed by the degree of substantive freedoms the institutions of education policy grant and not by competencies and skills predefined by multinational actors such as the World Bank. He illustrates how a neoliberal concept leads to focusing on a narrow set of educational outcomes that do not meet the needs of children, whereas a concept informed by the CA pays attention to the diversity and plurality of living conditions and life plans and hence to those dimensions that are relevant for the children's lives. The next contribution in this section also contrasts neoliberal and capabilities-oriented concepts. *Antoanneta Potsi* investigates beliefs and practices of Greek pre-primary teachers and asks whether they are oriented more towards performance or towards the capabilities of children. Her quantitative study shows that the teachers favour capability-based conceptions of schooling, although the new curriculum of teacher training focuses more on the insemination of school-oriented knowledge. She argues that teachers as front-line implementers should be involved in the development of educational reforms. The topic of third chapter in this section is the interaction of class and caste in the education processes of an Indian village. For his ethnographic study,

Lakshmi N. Venkataraman has revisited the small village of Sripuram – a village known from a famous study conducted by the Indian sociologist Andre Beteille in the 1960s. He combines the CA with the concept of intersectionality to grasp the complexity of an Indian reality shaped by diverse, sometimes contradictory interrelations of caste and class in the field of education.

The marginalized living situation of refugee children in Germany is the topic of the first contribution in the third section of this volume. In her qualitative interview study, *Franziska Eisenhuth* combines the CA with childhood studies and applies an operationalization of Martha Nussbaum's list of central human capabilities to the currently under-researched group of refugee children. This enables her to analyse both the limitations that these children face in Germany as well as the ways in which they develop agency in the frame of the given structures they live in. *Bettina Ritter* focuses on another group of marginalized young people in Germany, young mothers. She includes the CA as a research perspective into her biographical research study on young mothers who are obliged to participate in particular social service institutions. Her analysis leads her to conclude that welfare institutions try to force young mothers into functionings related to the 'normal life course' with a strong focus on integration into the labour market. What the young women experience is a strong tension between youth, labour work, and motherhood; and, from their own perspective, they lack the opportunity freedom to live the life of a young person without the obligation to deliver a certain prescribed outcome. In the final chapter, *Natalia Karmaeva* uses the CA to analyse the agency of young teaching academics in Germany by transferring the concept of human development to staff development at German universities. She investigates the framings these young academics construe for academic teaching – particularly in relation to research – and shows how these framings can constrain the young people in their professional development. Arguing that agency in the frame of the CA includes replacing existing practices that impede the realization of the common good with new ones that promote it, she draws the conclusion that self-reflection in the form of reframing the ideas of professional tasks leads to more agency and thus to a higher quality of work for young teaching academics.

The research projects show how the CA can be placed on a solid foundation through social science research, because this locates its normative framing in the context of social, cultural, economic, and other conditions and analyses these conditions in terms of which options they allow. However, social science research also benefits from this linkage, because it is grounded by the normative orientation of the CA towards freedom and basic capabilities. This collaboration brings societal change within reach – a change towards more social justice and the 'good life' for all.

References

Bourdieu, Pierre/Wacquant, Loïc J.D. (1992): An Invitation to Reflexive Sociology. Chicago: University of Chicago Press.
Khader, Serene J. (2011): Adaptive Preferences and Women's Empowerment. Oxford: Oxford University Press.
Nussbaum, Martha (2000): Women and Human Development: The Capabilities Approach. Cambridge: Cambridge University Press.
Nussbaum, Martha (2007): Frontiers of Justice. Disability, Nationality, Species Membership. 1st paperback edition. Cambridge: Harvard University Press.
Otto, Hans-Uwe/Ziegler, Holger (2013): Introduction: Enhancing Capabilities – the Role of Social Institutions. In: Otto, Hans-Uwe/Ziegler, Holger (eds.): Enhancing Capabilities. The Role of Institutions. Opladen/Farmington Hills: Barbara Budrich Publishers, pp. 7–9.
Ricoeur, Paul (2005): The Course of Recognition. Cambridge, Mass: Harvard University Press.
Robeyns, Ingrid (2005): The Capability Approach: a Theoretical Survey. In: Journal of Human Development, 6, 1, pp. 93–114.
Robeyns, Ingrid (2011): The Capability Approach. In: Zalta, Edward N. (ed.): The Stanford Encyclopedia of Philosophy. URL: http://plato.stanford.edu/archives/sum2011/entries /capability-approach/ – downloaded 01.05.2014.
Sayer, Andrew (2008): Who's Afraid of Critical Social Science? In: Current Sociology, 57, 6, pp. 767–786.
Sen, Amartya (1999): Development as Freedom. Oxford: Oxford University Press.
Zimmermann, Bénédicte (2006): Pragmatism and the Capability Approach. Challenges in Social Theory and Empirical Research. In: European Journal of Social Theory, 9, 4, pp. 467–484.

Conceptual Inquiries Into the Capability Approach

Rada Jancic

Intersubjectivity and Recognition in Serbian Primary Schools: The Contribution of Paul Ricœur to the Capability Approach

1 Introduction

Several theorists have addressed the concept of recognition in the context of educational institutions by looking at institutional mechanisms of recognition (Stojanov 2010) or various acts of recognition and misrecognition in classroom interaction (Blum 2001; Jonasson 2012). Apart from understanding recognition as a status-gaining activity (Fraser 2000; Honneth 1995), it is possible to elaborate this concept as a moral action of recognizing the "other" (Ricœur 2005a). Considering that teaching is understood as a moral activity (Fenstermacher 1990), recognition as a moral act can provide a new lens for comprehending interaction in educational institutions.

One possible way of understanding the teaching–studying–learning (TSL) process in the institutions of education is by interpreting it as a pedagogical interaction between the teacher and pupils. However, Kansanen (1999: 82) points out significantly that "all joint activity in teaching may be called interaction but all interaction is not pedagogical interaction". By this, he means that pedagogical interaction is defined as an activity with some content and also as a purposeful, intentional activity by the participants. Therefore, alongside the teacher and the pupil, the content of teaching and its purpose become the third element in this process. These three elements (teacher, pupil, and content) form a didactic triangle, and the interactions between them provide the context for creating a variety of relations: between teacher and pupil (pedagogical), between teacher and content, between pupil and content, and between teacher and pupil's learning (didactic) (Kansanen/Meri 1999; Toom 2006).

This chapter focuses on teachers' relations to self (professional and personal self), teachers' pedagogical relations (with pupils), and, to some extent, teachers' relation to the content of the teaching. These relations were investigated as part of a doctoral research project on capability-related subjective theories of primary school teachers in Serbia with the focus on critical incidents in classroom interaction. The aim is to explore teachers' understanding of recognizing the pupil as a capable human being and what pedagogical practices teachers employ in order to support or hinder the development of some of the pupils' capabilities. Five teachers first completed semi-structured interviews. Afterwards, they were interviewed while using video recordings of the lessons as stimuli to encourage reflection on critical incidents during teacher–pupil interaction.

There is good reason to focus on teachers' understanding of their relations in the classroom. Kansanen (1999) argues that interaction in the classroom is asymmetrical. The teacher usually has a position of power in teacher–pupil interaction, although these relations are not always as straightforward as they seem. Asymmetrical interaction implies that teacher and pupil do not have always the same intentions. The teacher's work, for example, is characterized by purposeful action. This means that teachers have a curricular purpose in mind when conducting an action; they have authority in this interaction; and, finally, they are legally obliged to guide the process (Kasanen 1999). On the other hand, for the pupils, the schools are places not only for learning but also for socialization in general. Accordingly, their intentions may not always be in line with those of the teacher, but might, for example, be dedicated to chatting with their peers rather than addressing the lesson task (Jonasson 2012).

Although there are critics of the asymmetrical relations in the classroom (e.g. Biesta 1994), Kansanen (1999) believes that asymmetry does not necessarily mean that these relations cannot be democratic. As van Manen (1990) points out, pedagogical interaction is characterized by attributes of asymmetrical relations: responsibility and dependency. This asymmetrical nature does not necessarily mean that teaching cannot be student-centred and that teachers do not recognize diverse pupils' characteristics and needs.

The aim of this chapter is to show how introducing Ricœur's concept of recognition can contribute to a better understanding of the pedagogical practices that teachers employ when they support or hinder the development of their pupils' capabilities. Therefore, I shall first present the framework used for analysing the teachers' verbal reports. It consists of the Capability Approach (CA) as a framework for just education and Ricœur's (2006) list of basic human capabilities. Special emphasis is placed on Ricœur's understanding of the concept of recognition. I shall start with a brief sketch of the study design. Then I shall present the analysis of teachers' verbal representations in order to develop my argumentation. I shall conclude with a few suggestions regarding how Paul Ricœur's phenomenology of the capable human being could contribute to some necessary strengthening of the CA and indicate some possible implications for research on classroom relations.

2 Human capabilities and recognition

The theoretical foundations for this study are two approaches that have been found to be complementary. The CA is used as a broad framework for understanding just education that places emphasis on not only the "functionings" but also the "capabilities" of a person to achieve valuable beings and doings (Unterhalter 2009). This approach is complemented by Paul Ricœur's *phenomenology of the capable human being*. In this study, the CA provides the normative framework for understanding just education (the one that focuses not only on the functionings but also on the capabilities of pupils) and gives a broader political framework for understanding pupils' capabilities in the institutions of education. Ricœur gives a moral framework of the capabilities and provides a mechanism for developing them: recognition. Situating the analysis in this framework, it is possible to shed some light on how recognition is manifested in teachers' everyday pedagogical practices, how it affects and defines the relations in the TSL process and how it affects teachers' development of pupils' capabilities.

In order to discuss why and how these two approaches have been implemented in the analysis of pedagogical interaction in Serbian primary schools, I will introduce some of their basic ideas and concepts such as: capabilities, functionings, conversion factor and agency.

2.1 The Capability Approach: the basic concepts

Both the CA and Ricœur's phenomenology are based on the concept of *capability*, understanding it in a somewhat different manner. In the CA, the term *capability* is distinguished from the term *functionings* because they, according to Sen (1980), present potential for achievement of functionings. Functionings constitute achieved capabilities (e.g. working or being healthy) – beings and doings or the outcome of the opportunities that a person had at her or his disposal. For example, reading is considered a functioning, but a person should have capabilities to develop this functioning, such as being taught how to read or having books at her or his disposal (Walker/Unterhalter 2007). More often than not, the functionings are at the centre of attention in policymaking and evaluation programmes. They are prescribed paternalistically by policymakers who expect every member of the society to achieve the same specific functioning. Policy development is therefore a very significant concept in the CA, arguing that policy interventions should focus not only on functionings but also on the capabilities that provide people with the possibility to make valuable choices. Although the practice of prescribed functionings is criticized, it is, however, relevant for children. Various theorists argue that children need to achieve certain capabilities by focusing on their functionings (Biggeri 2007; Nussbaum 2000).

The CA introduced *conversion factors* as another important concept. Robeyns (2005) defines these as factors that influence how free the person is in translating resources into functionings, and she distinguishes three different types of *conversion factors*: personal, social, and environmental. She gives examples of several conversion factors,[1] but in order to fully appreciate their potential, it is necessary to explore more concretely what factors enable a person to transfer resources into functionings. In this study, it is understood that recognition can act as a conversion factor in the pedagogical interaction. This argument will be illustrated through the analysis of teachers' accounts.

Finally, the concept of *agency* is also especially relevant in educational research. It represents the idea that a person is an active and reflective agent rather than a passive recipient. An example of this in educational research is student-centred education. In line with this, Walker and Unterhalter (2007) point out that learners are not just the agents of their own learning; they are also recipients of the agency of other people such as teachers or peers. Therefore, they significantly pose the question whether "in considering agency [...] different learners are recognized socially and educationally as having equal claims on resources and opportunities" (Walker/Unterhalter 2007: 6). A pupil's opportunity to be an agent is therefore of significant interest when discussing the issue of agency in the institutions of education. In contrast, there is a lack of research that explores issues of teachers' agency (Day et al. 2006; Tao 2013). However, I shall show that the way this topic emerged in the data analysis indicates that it needs to be addressed as a significant theme.

Although the concepts of capabilities, functionings, conversion factors, and agency are valuable when conceptualizing the social provision that enables dignified human life, the CA has its weak points that need improvement. In her seminal theoretical survey of the CA, Robeyns (2005) lists the most common critiques based on the claims that the approach is too individualistic and does not pay sufficient attention to groups and social structures. She persuasively explains that the CA is based on ethical rather than ontological or methodological individualism (Robeyns 2005: 107ff.). This means that the individuals should be the main focus of the policies and the only way to improve human well-being is to count each person as an end and not as a means. Although Robeyns gives examples of various theorists who refer to the importance of groups and social structures, she acknowledges that in this respect, the CA should be improved. In order to introduce the significance of social groups into the discussion on the development of capabilities, I have turned to representatives of continental philosophy, more concretely to Paul

---

[1] Just to name a few: personal: sex; social: gender; environmental: climate.

Ricœur's (Ricœur 1994, 2005b) *phenomenology of the capable human being* and especially his concept of *recognition*.

2.2 Ricœur's *l'homme capable*

To describe the disparities of notions to which Ricœur has given thought and especially to present a systematic coherence in his approach to philosophy would be a daunting task. He contributed to the notions of subjectivity, liberty, language, narrative, time, history, suffering, justice, and so forth. Ricœur's ability to engage in intellectual dialogues with various opposing approaches produced an intriguing and inspiring corpus of ideas (Kaplan 2008).

Despite having many other intellectual interests, Ricœur dedicated most of his long and productive career to the development of his *phenomenology of the capable human being*. One could say that throughout his works, from "Freedom and Nature" (1966)[2] to "The Course of Recognition" (2005b), one can find the notion of the capable human being (*l'homme capable*) expressed through various modes of "I can" statements: "I can speak", "I can act", "I can tell", and finally "I can be responsible". These "I can" statements also imply that a person who utters them has not only the capacity but also the freedom to speak, act, and tell.

Ricœur argues that the term *capability* is connected to the notion of self-recognition. Defining the word capability, Ricœur ascribes it to the human action that denotes "the kind of power that we claim to be able to exercise". So he proposes "a minimal definition of capability as the power to cause something to happen" and where this power is prone to self-recognition (Ricœur 2006: 17f.). It is worth noting that the term *capability* is defined loosely leaving plenty of room for interpretations. Paul Ricœur uses the term *capability* synonymously with the term *capacity*, whereas Sen (1999), for example, understands *capability* to be *freedom*.

Following the interpretation proposed by Honerød Hoveid and Hoveid (2009), *the phenomenology of the capable human being* could be an informative framework for understanding the development of pupils' capabilities in educational settings. Put briefly, these capabilities are:

- *Capability to speak*: the first and basic capacity of the person – being able to use the pronoun "I" and opening up the possibility for the identification of an individual. In teacher–student interaction, this would mean that there is an "I–you" relation that can be violated if the pupil is never singled out from the group of his or her classmates.

---

2   The original French edition of the book "Freedom and Nature" was first published in 1950.

- *Capability to act*: "to make something happen", referring to the "who" structure of the action: "Who did it?" This again relates to the attribution of the action to a person. In the educational process, it relates to the idea of giving more space to pupils to initiate the action. As Honerød Hoveid and Hoveid (2009) understand it, this assumes not only prescriptive actions initiated by the teachers in which pupils will give "the right" answers, which is common for educational settings. Development of this capability would imply situations in which teachers are interlocutors, and in which they become "the other in the process of learning".[3]
- *Capability to tell*: Ricœur connects the idea of narrating to the notion of identity by arguing that personal identity can be defined as narrative identity. With my narration, I state myself and my life as a social human being, as a participant in interpersonal relations.
- *Capability of imputation*: by acquiring all three previously mentioned capacities, it is possible for a person to be capable of imputation. This suggests that a person has the capacity to be responsible for his or her actions (Honerød Hoveid/Hoveid 2009:463–467).

According to Ricœur (2005b), when a person is recognized as the individual actor and an action is attributed to that specific person, he or she becomes capable of imputation: of responsibility for the committed action. In other words, through identification of oneself, recognition by others, being a capable human being, having the capacity to speak one's identity, initiating action, and narrating one's personal history (that is at the same time part of the collective history), an individual becomes capable of imputation. This capability is obtained through mutual recognition with others. The action is attributed to a person by him or herself and by others, and that is what gives this person the capacity to be responsible for his or her action. It is very important here to note that the term *responsibility* is seen here as a moral concept rather than a juridical notion.

Nussbaum (2000: 78) emphasizes that in order to be capable, human beings must live with dignity. However, it is justifiable to assume that a person must be assigned the status of a dignified human being by societal practices. What Ricœur (2005b) claims is that in order to be assigned this status, a person needs to be recognized by the oneself and others as a dignified human being.

---

3   As mentioned earlier, there are debates about the equally distributed organization of teacher–pupil interactions. Aside from the critiques, there are also strong arguments that support and justify this nature of the relationship (see, e.g. Kansanen 1999; Van Manen 1990).

2.3 On recognition

Various recognition theorists and moral philosophers (Fraser 2000; Honneth 1995; Stojanov 2007) emphasize the significance of social and political recognition in the lives of a person. Fraser (2000) and Honneth (1995) emphasize political recognition and status-gaining mechanisms and especially contemplate the problem of misrecognition and the conflicts that arise from it. There are various discussions on the concept of recognition in the context of educational institutions (Stojanov 2007, 2010). Stojanov (2010), influenced by Honneth's writings, for example, points out that the goal of educational policies should be to institutionalize forms of recognition in all areas of educational provision. He claims that by implementing different forms of recognition, students would be enabled to engage in the process of self-development and world-disclosing and by that to accomplish the mission of *Bildung*.

Ricœur (2005b) takes a slightly different course in developing his philosophy of recognition, starting from a lexicographical survey of the word "recognition". He continues with this transformation of the meaning and moves from recognition–identification to recognition of oneself and finalizes this with the notion of intersubjective recognition. He ties the concept of recognition to the notion of *l'homme capable* and regards it as a symbolic gesture that depends on the moral responsibilities of a person. Therefore he does not advocate institutionalization.

When receiving the John W. Kluge Prize for Lifetime Achievement in the Human Sciences in 2004, Paul Ricœur (2005a) indicatively gave a title to his speech "Becoming Capable, Being Recognized", pointing out that the one is bound to the other. But, one might ask, what does it mean to be recognized in a Ricœurian sense? In his book, "The course of recognition", Ricœur (2005b) identifies three phases of recognition:

- *Recognition–identification:*
  Ricœur commences the elaboration of the recognition as identification of the one who is not oneself, the one who is different. He importantly points out that "being distinguished and identified is what the humiliated person aspires to" (Ricœur 2005b: 25). However, he continues and complements this statement with understanding the recognition by joining a specific group and recognizing a person as a member of a specific group.
- *Recognition of oneself:*
  However, in order to reach the point of mutual recognition, Ricœur states that it is necessary for a person first to recognize "oneself". This self-recognition is implied through the statement "I believe that I can". This statement also assumes what Ricœur addressed as the confidence a person has in his or her power to act and the power of the "other" to act or, in

other words, *agency* (Ricœur 2005b: 134). However, his notion of *self* is relational. It is not possible to know oneself without the relation with the "other", and therefore an individual is developed through mutual recognition.[4]

- *Intersubjective recognition:*
Ricœur (2005b) points out significantly that the recognition of oneself cannot be achieved without intersubjectivity. In other words, without the affirmative recognition of others, there is no possibility for "me" to know more about myself and others. This acknowledgment is achieved through self-reflection, because Ricœur takes the viewpoint of an individual and elaborates intersubjectivity in that manner. However, he does not just understand intersubjectivity as defining oneself and defining the other. Within this notion, he assumes understanding of the others as subjects and understanding of oneself as another (Ricœur 1994).

3 Inquiry into the Primary School Teachers' Accounts

This chapter is based on a doctoral research project on the capability-related subjective theories of primary school teachers in Serbia. The main research question guiding the investigation is related to discovering what subjective theories primary school teachers have about recognizing a pupil as a "capable human being". In order to gain more information on the capability-related pedagogical practice of primary school teachers, it was also necessary to ask how teachers enhance or hinder the development of pupils' capabilities in the process of teacher–pupil interaction.

Data for this study consists of 28 interviews and observation notes collected from five primary school teachers in the north of Serbia. Data-gathering methods included observation of the lessons, a semi-structured initial interview with teachers ($N = 5$), and videotapes of lessons that were then used for video-stimulated recall interviews ($N = 23$). Videotaped lessons were first observed by the researcher who singled out critical incidents for discussion with the teacher.

The broad theoretical framework presented in the previous section had been set before entering the field. Practically, this meant that selection of the incidents was based on:

---

4   This notion is very close to George Herbert Mead's theory of socialization. Mead advocates that a person's self-image is formed in interaction with others and understanding how others see us ("taking the role of the other").

- The way pupils were addressed (as a group, individual, by name, nickname, surname) by the teacher, calling out mechanisms in the classroom, reactions to pupils' inputs, touch and/or body language of the teacher.
- If and when pupils had the opportunity to initiate the action and situations in which this would occur.
- If pupils had the opportunity to narrate their personal stories (if they were stopped or allowed to tell, and in what situations this happened).
- Finally, some incidents that did not belong to the theoretical framework, but in some way presented a break in the lesson flow that the teacher needed to resolve. These situations were used as stimuli for discussion with teachers due to their unusual character.

Five participating teachers reflected on 129 critical incidents in 23 video-stimulated recall interviews during which I asked them first to try to describe and then to explain or justify the reasons for taking that decision and acting in a specific manner during the lesson interaction. The aim was to reconstruct teachers' subjective theories about some of the pedagogical practices they apply during the TSL process of classroom interaction. The argumentation in this chapter is based on these verbal responses by teachers.

4 Intersubjectivity and recognition in classroom interaction

Applying Ricœur's *l'homme capable* as a lens for observing the educational practice that enhances or hinders the development of pupils' capabilities also suggests taking into account the recognition mechanisms that do (or do not) exist in classroom interaction. This pedagogical sensitivity, manifesting in the form of recognizing a child's diverse needs and identities, provides a solid basis for the academic aspect of schooling (Van Manen 1991).

When translating these statements to educational settings, one can reflect on the interpersonal relationships in the classroom and observe them on the basis of "intentional community" (Hoveid/Honerød Hoveid 2008) in which value is placed on practising intersubjective recognition that enables mutual understanding of intent. However, this conceptualization also assumes that children are recognized as reasoning agents similar to the way adults are recognized (Biggeri 2007; Stables 2008).

In this study, teachers' accounts of the critical incidents in the classroom interaction revealed their relation to self and their pedagogical relation to their pupils. Some of the themes that emerged within these relations were: *teacher's agency*, *pedagogical well-being*, *pedagogical authority*, and *peda-*

gogical care of pupils. This chapter focuses on the last theme because, according to the teachers' accounts, what is understood in the theory as "developing capabilities" is understood by the teachers as activities that are part of their pedagogical care of pupils. In addition, this professional role of caregiver also affected the other aspects of teaching such as well-being and agency.

4.1 Recognizing the "capable other"

The following examples of teachers' verbal representations are moments of teacher–pupil interaction that reflect the childrearing character of schooling and reveal the teacher as caregiver. Following Ricœur's (2005b) argumentation, it is assumed that in these moments of interaction, recognizing the "capable other" is necessary for establishing a relationship of mutual recognition that assumes a good understanding of the intent of action. But being inspired by Amartya Sen, Ricœur acknowledges that some capabilities are not just needed but required. One of the teachers states the following:

> First and utmost is to gain certain trust, mutual trust between teacher and a child. I won't say pupil on purpose, but exactly a child, as a child, as a person. (KLARA,[5] 1st-grade teacher)

The teacher in this example is trying to emphasize the holistic perspective of a pupil, expanding the understanding of his or her comprehensive identity: identity as a child. Klara is grounding her relationship with the pupil on this attempt to gain a comprehensive understanding of the child. This statement also assumes that Klara identifies each child as an individual. She uses the singular form when explaining classroom practice, referring to one child at a time. However, she refers to herself only in the form of a professional self, thereby presenting another example of the asymmetrical nature of the teacher–pupil relation. It is a relationship between the teacher on one side, which is only one of the possible roles of a teacher, and a child on the other side, as wholeness. The teacher practises recognition identification by viewing the pupil as a person. Further, she also tries to use this recognition–identification to move towards establishing a balanced intersubjectivity represented in the form of trust.

Moreover, this example reveals one attempt of a teacher to develop the capability of affiliation (Nussbaum 2000). Nussbaum (2000: 79) defined this capability as "being able to live with and toward others, to recognize and show concern for other human beings, to engage in various forms of social interaction". However, what is needed in order to enhance development of

---

5　The names of teachers used in this chapter are pseudonyms.

this capability is intersubjectivity. As Ricœur (2005b) argues, through intersubjectivity, a person relates to the self and to the other, recognizing one's and other person's capabilities. Even in asymmetrical relations such as these in which the teacher relates only to the pupil as a whole in the role of the professional self, enhancing the capability of affiliation arose as a foundation for establishing pedagogical relations in the TSL process.

This recognition identification of a pupil as a person can be observed as a *social conversion factor* that enables a translation of the resources of teacher's intent into the functionings of balanced relations in the classroom interaction.

Further following the argument, it is assumed that by setting up a relationship of trust, teacher and pupil establish a mutual recognition of intent. The pupil acknowledges that the teacher has good intentions by placing his or her trust in the teacher. By obtaining trust, the teacher is provided with an authority to perform the professional tasks. As for the child, he or she will become able to benefit from being enabled to develop the capabilities necessary for human flourishing. This is how the same teacher reasons while describing one of the classroom situations:

I use their life experiences, and through that I try to give some suggestion, indiscernible, so you won't violate their privacy but give some suggestion as to how they can alter themselves as personalities. (KLARA, 1st-grade teacher)

The previous quote shows how Klara emphasized the establishment of mutual trust between herself as a teacher and a child. She uses this mutual recognition of intent to fulfil her role of a caregiver. This assumes that a child has developed a relationship of trust and recognizes that the teacher has certain intentions, certain tasks to fulfil. Based on this recognition, a child opens a possibility for a teacher to be in the position to give advice. This trust also plays a role in justifying the asymmetrical nature of the teacher–pupil interaction and granting it validity. Klara tries to influence the development of a child; and by giving suggestions, she also provides choices in the form of alternative patterns of action or development.

Similar findings can be found in earlier research. Harjunen (2009, 2011) argues that not only teachers need to recognize the needs of pupils and respond to them appropriately, but also pupils need to recognize the intent of the teacher and to give their consent to the teacher's authority. In this case, mutual recognition of *intentionality* represents a basis for establishing an authoritative teaching practice that enables balanced, although still asymmetrical, pedagogical relations in the classroom.

Furthermore, Klara here mentions another capability that she is obviously aware of implicitly. That is the capability of being free from shame (Sen 1999) or as Nussbaum (2000: 79) puts it "having the social bases of self-respect and non-humiliation" as manifested in the teacher's statement "so you won't violate their privacy". Through recognition in the form of distinguishing the child as a person who has privacy that needs to be recognized, the teacher enables and supports one of the basic capabilities of affiliation.

Even though educational institutions are considered to have great potential for enhancing capabilities, regardless of whether they are observed in a Ricœurian sense or within the framework of CA (Brighouse 2000; Nussbaum 2000), schools are not always the places in which pupils' capabilities can flourish (Honerød Hoveid/Hoveid 2009; Unterhalter 2003). Moreover, as Unterhalter (2003) reports, schools can be places of capability deprivation.

4.2 Misrecognition as impediment

Honerød Hoveid and Hoveid (2009) emphasize that schools are not places in which personal narrative is endorsed. And, according to Ricœur (2005b), personal self is narrative self that manifests in a person's capacity to narrate her or his life history. Indeed, most teachers in this study accepted verbal inputs from pupils in cases of teacher–pupil interaction only when those inputs were justified by the purpose of the lesson.

The following incident occurred during the lesson when a pupil approached the teacher while she was addressing the whole class. The pupil attempted to say something to the teacher while pointing to his leg, but the teacher sent the pupil back to his seat, telling him with a smile that they would discuss this later. The teacher was later shown the recording of this incident, and she was asked to reflect on this situation. Here is one of the explanations that she gave for her reaction:

That is the moment that, that really puts you off track. ESPECIALLY[6] I mind when we are doing something serious. Look, you are explaining the task and he comes with that kind of a story: *Teacher, you know, I fell today.* It really impedes me! It really impedes me! (MARIA 2nd-grade teacher)

In this example, the teacher differentiates between the "serious" content of the lesson and the pupil's narrative that is, within this understanding, not serious but trivial. It is to be expected that teachers need to have the curriculum in their minds and focus on the lesson content (Kansanen 2000). However, one can observe here the absence of recognition of intent: conflicting intentions between the teacher and the pupil. In this situation, the pupil failed to recognize the teacher's intent to deliver a lecture to the whole class. On the other hand, due to the purposeful nature of the teacher's actions, this teacher

---

6   Emphasis by the teacher.

reacts to enable the flow of the lesson and bear in mind the purpose of the curriculum. Therefore, she is not in a position to respond to this input and has to discourage this pupil's attempt to narrate.

It is also interesting to notice in what way the teacher here is affected by these verbal and non-verbal actions of pupils. The teacher is not just affected by it on a professional level in her form of the professional self, but Maria gives an impression that her personal self is also affected by this when she repeats "It really impedes me!"

Both the teacher's professional and personal self are being affected by these interaction moments. It is possible to see how these situations can impede the teacher's personal self in the following example in which a teacher is reflecting on an incident in which one pupil spat at another during the lesson. She says:

If you want to do everything well, and you really try, it can be sometimes very difficult. Sometimes it happens that I am not in the mood, or you have some personal problem or family problem that you carry with yourself, or you are ill, and then they [pupils] sometimes just crush you. And then someone comes with this spitting or something so ridiculous that you just want to scream. (ANA, 3rd-grade teacher)

Here one can see that the teacher's intentionality to deliver the teaching to the best of her abilities is being obstructed by either her pupils' behaviour or her own personal state, and this is a cause of great frustration. Ana mentions the feeling of being "crushed" or wanting to scream. It indicates that Ana's *pedagogical well-being*[7] in these moments is poor, as seen in the lack of the agency she is displaying. In this sequence, she leaves the impression of being helpless and powerless to act meaningfully. Here, the teacher is not the acting agent but rather the recipient of the pupils' agency. Conflicting intentions in the teacher and pupil lead to the misrecognition of the *intent*, thereby disturbing the balanced pedagogical relations in the TLS process and also affecting the power relations that are inherent to teacher–pupil interaction.

5 Conclusion

I have tried to combine two theoretical understandings of capabilities and show how they manifest in the everyday pedagogical practices of primary school teachers: the CA and Ricœur's *phenomenology of the capable human*

---

[7] Pedagogical well-being is understood here in the way suggested by Soini et al. (2010) who describe it as occupational well-being in the teaching–studying–learning process within the school community.

being. Ricœur is clearly a representative of continental philosophy. Although he discusses his philosophical approach from the point of view of an individual in his understanding of capabilities (Ricœur 1994, Ricœur 2005b, Ricœur 2005a, Ricœur 2006), he argues that the phenomena of capabilities and recognition are at least to some extent determined by the community/group. The personal dimension is embedded in the historical and cultural context in which a personal narrative is part of the wider communal heritage. Ricœur's strong relation to the community and the intersubjectivity of every person inspired, for example, Dauenhauer (2010) to name Ricœur's understanding of justice "communitarian liberalism". With these foundations, Ricœur can complement Sen and Nussbaum, the most prominent developers of the CA, who, as representatives of the Anglo-American tradition, emphasize the individuals as ends of every policy action.

In this chapter, I have examined the possibility of strengthening the CA by introducing the concept of recognition as a *social conversion factor*. This implies that recognition enables a translation of resources into valuable functionings. It is very important to note here that recognition understood in such a manner does not imply legal and institutional recognition, but rather moral activity of the actors. Based on the analysis of the teachers' responses to some moments of teacher–pupil interaction, one can observe that the recognition of the other, of the needs and intents of the other, can serve as basis for establishing a relationship of trust, teacher's pedagogical well-being, and balanced classroom relations.

Finally, I would like to conclude by pointing out that teachers show recognition of certain capabilities in their pupils and not just their identities. Considering the CA, these are the capability of affiliation and the capability of being free from shame. In a Ricœurian sense, teachers recognize the capability to speak. In this recognition, one can observe the important step forward in understanding the value of recognition as a conversion factor. Recognition of capabilities brings in the idea of acknowledging other person's freedoms to achieve various beings and doings. This moves away from the notion of identity and focuses attention on the recognition of the freedoms every person should have in order to make informed choices about the life he or she values. In the provision of education, it would assume that although focusing on pupils' functioning is very important in the development of children's capabilities, it is necessary to recognize pupils' capabilities of speaking, acting, and narrating – leading to the recognition of moral responsibility. In understanding the ideas of just education, it could be valuable to further investigate these pedagogical relations in terms of recognition and capabilities.

References

Biesta, Gert (1994): Education as practical intersubjectivity. Towards a critical pragmatic understanding of education. In: Educational Theory, 44, 3, pp. 299–317.
Biggeri, Mario (2007): Children's Valued Capabilities. In: Walker, Melanie/Unterhalter, Elaine (eds.): Amartya Sen's capability approach and social justice in education. New York: Pelgrave Macmillan, pp. 197–214.
Blum, Lawrence (2001): Recognition and Multiculturalism in Education. In: Journal of the Philosophy of Education, 35, 4, pp. 539–559.
Brighouse, Harry (2000): School Choice and Social Justice. Oxford University Press.
Dauenhauer, Bernard (2010): Ricœur and Political Theory: liberalism and communitarianism. In: Davidson, Scott: Ricœur across the Disciplines. New York/London: Continuum, pp. 102–121.
Day, Christopher/Kington, Alison/Stobart, Gordon/Sammons, Pam (2006): The Personal and Professional Selves of Teachers: stable and unstable identities. In: British Educational Research Journal, 32, 4, pp. 601–616.
Fenstermacher, Gary (1990): Some Moral Considerations on Teaching as a Profession. In: Goodlad, John I./Soder, Roger/Sirotnik, Kenneth A. (eds.): The Moral Dimensions of Teaching. San Francisco: Jossey Bass Publishers, pp. 130–151.
Fraser, Nancy (2000): Rethinking Recognition. In: New Left Review, 3, pp. 107–120.
Harjunen, Elina (2009): How Do Teachers View Their Own Pedagogical Authority? In: Teachers and Teaching: theory and practice, 15, 1, pp. 109–129.
Harjunen, Elina (2011): Students' Consent to a Teacher's Pedagogical Authority. In: Scandinavian Journal of Educational Research, 55, 4, pp. 403–424.
Honneth, Axel (1995): The Struggle for Recognition: the moral grammar of social conflicts. Cambridge, Massachusetts: The MIT Press.
Hoveid, Halvor/Hoveid, Marit Honerød (2008): Teachers' Identity, Self and the Process of Learning. In: Studies in Philosophy and Education, 27, pp. 125–136.
Hoveid, Marit Honerød/ Hoveid, Halvor (2009): Educational Practice and Development of Human Capabilities. In: Studies in Philosophy and Education, 28, pp. 461–472.
Jonasson, Charlotte (2012): Teachers and Students' Divergent Perceptions of Student Engagement: recognition of school or workplace goals. In: British Journal of Sociology of Education, 33, 5, pp. 723–741.
Kansanen, Pertti (1999): Teaching as Teaching-Studying-Learning Interaction. In: Scandinavian Journal of Educational Research, 43, 1, pp. 81–89.
Kansanen, Pertti (2000): Teachers' Pedagogical Thinking. Theoretical landscapes, practical challenges. New York: Peter Lang.
Kansanen, Pertti/Meri, Matti (1999): The Didactic Relation in the Teaching-Studying-Learning Process. In: TNTEE publications, 2, 1, pp. 107–116.
Kaplan, David M. (2008): Introduction: reading Ricœur. In: Kaplan, David M.: Reading Ricœur. Albany: State University of New York Press, pp. 1–12.
Nussbaum, Martha C. (2000): Women and Human Development. The capabilities approach. Cambridge, New York: Cambridge University Press.
Ricœur, Paul (1966): Freedom and Nature: the voluntary and involuntary. Evanston, Illinois: Northwestern University Press.
Ricœur, Paul (1994): Oneself as Another. Chicago: University of Chicago Press.

Ricœur, Paul (2005a): Becoming Capable, Being Recognizes. Text Kluge Prize. Washington (unpubl.).

Ricœur, Paul (2005b): The Course of Recognition. Cambridge, Mass.: Harvard University Press.

Ricœur, Paul (2006): Capabilities and Rights. In: Deneulin, Séverine/Nebel, Mathias/Sagovsky, Nicholas (eds.): Transforming Unjust Structures. Dordrecht: Springer, pp. 17–26.

Robeyns, Ingrid (2005): The Capabilities Approach: a theoretical survey. In: Journal of Human Development, 6, 1, pp. 93–117.

Sen, Amartya (1980): Equality of What? In: McMurrin, Sterling M. (ed.): The Tanner Lectures on Human Values. Salt Lake City: University of Utah Press, pp. 197–220.

Sen, Amartya (1999): Development of Freedom. Oxford, New York: Oxford University Press.

Soini, Tiina/ Pyhältö, Kirsi/ Pietarinen, Janne (2010): Pedagogical Well-being: reflecting learning and well-being in teachers' work. In: Teachers and Teaching: theory and practice, 16, 6, pp. 735–751.

Stables, Andrew (2008): Childhood and the Philosophy of Education. An anti-Aristotelian perspective. London, New York: Continuum International Pub.

Stojanov, Krassimir (2007): Intersubjective Recognition and the Development of Propositional Thinking. In: Journal of Philosophy of Education, 41, pp. 75–93.

Stojanov, Krassimir (2010): Overcoming Social Pathologies in Education: on the concepts of respect in R. S. Peters and Axel Honneth. In: Journal of Philosophy of Education, 43, 161–172.

Tao, Sharon (2013): Why are Teachers Absent? Utilising the capabilities approach and critical realism to explain teacher performance in Tanzania. In: International Journal of Educational Development, 33, 1, pp. 2–14.

Toom, Auli (2006): Tacit Pedagogical Knowing: at the core of teacher's professionality. Diss. Helsinki: University of Helsinki.

Unterhalter, Elaine (2003): The Capabilities Approach and Gendered Education: an examination of South African complexities. In: Theory and Research in Education, 1, 1, pp. 7–22.

Unterhalter, Elaine (2009): Education. In: Deneulin, Séverine/Shahani, Lila: An Introduction to the Human Development and Capability Approach. Freedom and Agency. Sterling/Ottawa: International Development Research Centre, pp. 207–227.

Van Manen, Max (1990): Beyond Assumptions: shifting the limits of action research. In: Theory into Practice, 25, 3, pp. 152–157.

Van Manen, Max (1991): The Tact of Teaching: the meaning of pedagogical thoughtfulness. Albany: State University of New York Press.

Walker, Melanie/Unterhalter, Elaine (2007): The Capability Approach: Its potential for work in education. In: Walker, Melanie/Unterhalter, Elaine (eds.): Amartya Sen's Capability Approach and Social Justice in Education. New York: Palgrave Macmillan, pp. 1–18.

Erika Bozzato

The Contribution of Critical Discourse Analysis to the Capability Approach in Education Policy Analysis: The Case of Kosovo

1 Introduction

After the end of the conflict in 1999, education in Kosovo underwent massive reforms that simultaneously tackled policy, infrastructures, administration, staff, teaching methodologies, and materials. The reforms were part of a much larger state-building process, ultimately managed by the UNMIK (United Nation Interim Administration Mission in Kosovo) with the support of other international organizations. Its aims were to perform administrative functions, coordinate humanitarian interventions, and eventually create structures and conditions for the takeover of local authorities, which happened in 2002 with the creation of the Ministry of Education, Science and Technology of Kosovo (MEST). Since the conflict, copious funds have been channelled into the education field through either governmental development agencies, intergovernmental organizations, or NGOs, with support being given to virtually all sectors and particular attention being paid to curriculum development, teacher training, special education, and the Education Management and Information System (EMIS). Selected *lead agencies* were responsible for both the delivery of services and capacity building in that specific sector (Sommers/Buckland 2004: 78). These were UNICEF, the CIDA[1]-sponsored Kosovo Education Development Programme (KEDP), the Finnish Support for the Development of Education in Kosovo (FSDEK), and the World Bank. However, the role of education in Kosovo remains politically charged and controversial, and is highly influenced by political and ethnic animosities. Since the 1990s, two parallel systems of education have been present in the territory, one run by the Kosovo-Albanian authorities – then Kosovo government – in Pristina and the other by the Serbian government in Belgrade; and the multitude of actors involved have very different and sometimes divergent standpoints (Sommers/Buckland 2005: 38). International organizations gained substantial power (Barlett et al. 2004), and under the pressure of achieving quick results, rapid reforms were pushed through with the help of

1   Canadian International Development Agency

international consultants, leaving little space for local expertise and for a well-planned handover process, and working more with political personalities rather than local educators.

Although post-conflict reconstruction of education shows considerable progress, access to education and learner retention, especially for minorities, the rural population, and children with special needs are still an issue (Sommers/Buckland 2005: 38). Two different systems are still operating, and schooling is virtually ethnically segregated (Sommers/Buckland 2005: 38) with not all communities being provided with curricula and textbooks in their own native language. It has been recognized that most of the international organizations that flooded into Kosovo were neither sufficiently aware nor took enough time to get acquainted with the field and its specific issues – also due to their specific structures and high turnover (Sommers/Buckland 2004, 2005). From the local side, resistance to international initiatives was also generated at times (Bache/Taylor 2003). This also contributed to creating a substantial gap between the intentions stated in both legislation and policy documents and their actual implementation. It can be claimed that some of the premises underlying the conflict are still in place, and that a thorough investigation of the social context and of the relations among the actors involved becomes paramount if existing education policies are to improve.

Assessing and evaluating education policy established in such a setting requires a framework that takes into account the consequences or the restrictions that this policy may have for people's well-being. A close analysis of the context – including the social structures and actors involved – and the origin of policy can provide not only a crucial understanding but also instruments for change. The Capability Approach (CA) is being used as an evaluative framework for educational policies (Robeyns 2006: 368) as well as a framework for criticizing social norms and discourses that may restrict people's capabilities and ultimately social justice. CA is a useful theoretical framework, because it focuses on individuals' real freedom and expansion of possibilities. Melanie Walker (2003: 168) argues that the goal of social justice is to promote not only individual but also collective flourishing. Education may, in fact, contribute not only to social reproduction but also to social transformation, enabling learners to use their critical skills to ameliorate the social context in which they live (Walker 2003: 169). This highlights the need to assess educational policies in their context of implementation in order to see how they can improve society and what kind of knowledge they produce (Walker 2003: 170). But despite being recognized as largely influential (Nussbaum 1996, 2007; Robeyns 2005), the functions of context and sociocultural setting in the creation of the capability set and individual choice are not conceptualized in depth within the CA. Nonetheless, investigating the context and structures in which capabilities are nested is especially relevant in policy analysis, given the fact that social determinants, including social context and social structure, are the fields in which social change interventions are possible, hardly involving the capabilities directly. Moreover, issues of power are also quite disregarded in the CA, and as a consequence, any resulting policy evaluation and assessment may be incomplete or deceptive.

In contrast, the social context and issues of power in their different aspects are constitutive aspects of Critical Discourse Analysis (CDA) in which social life in its different aspects can be considered as an interconnected network of social practices. The function of CDA is to investigate the role of the discourses within social practice in relation to the other elements, and, at the same time, to unveil power relations. CA, in contrast, as an ethical individualistic theory, bases its evaluation on individuals, whereas CDA struggles to report consequences of dominant discourse and power at a generic individual level, and to give a definition of *well-being*.

Therefore, the present chapter tackles two issues of policy analysis: the relation between the individual and the social context along with the power relations underlying a given society. I shall argue that CDA could make an important contribution to the analysis of the context within which the individual's capability set is generated and to the issues of social power. CDA could also back up CA when assessing or analysing policies, especially in their discursive parts (Apthorpe/Gasper 1996; Gasper 2000; Robeyns 2006). In particular, I shall show this in the case of the reform of education policy in Kosovo.

2 Role of the social context in the Capability Approach

The CA has been defined as a "broad normative framework for the evaluation and assessment of individual well-being and social arrangements, the design of policies and proposals about social change in society" (Robeyns 2005: 94). Although the CA does not provide the theoretical basis to explain poverty, inequality, or well-being, it does offer a framework to conceptualize and evaluate these phenomena (Robeyns 2005: 94). Applying the CA to issues of policy and social change will therefore often require the addition of explanatory theories (Robeyns 2005: 94). Amartya Sen, who first developed the approach (Sen 1980, 1984), claims that policy evaluation should ideally concentrate on people's capabilities, and on removing obstacles that could prevent the fulfilment of their personal choices. Capabilities are in fact conceived as a set of possibilities that may be further translated into actual conditions or actions called *functionings*. The difference between functionings and capabilities is between what a person *does* realize and the set of potential options she or he has had.

The formation of the capability set and the conversion into achieved functionings is influenced by a number of variables and relations including social structures and institutions (Gasper 2002; Robeyns 2005; Sen 2002; Stewart/Deneulin 2002). Social context and structures are taken into account and integrated when conceptualizing people's capability sets in more than one way:

a. Social context can influence the capability set through individual conversion factors
b. Social context can influence the capability set directly
c. Social context and public debates can/should influence the definition of capability sets

2.1 Social context and conversion factors

The importance of social context and structures has been highlighted in a number of papers by both Sen and Nussbaum when responding to claims that CA does not pay enough attention to groups and social structures (including institutions), but rather focuses too much on individuals (Robeyns 2005).[2] In fact, individualism in the CA (Gasper 2002) together with the critique of CA's limited consideration of relations between individuals and social structures (Ibrahim 2006) have been a matter of controversy. The CA is an ethical individualistic theory, but it is not ontological (Robeyns 2003). This means that capabilities and functionings are properties of individuals and that their evaluation will be based on individuals and not on households or communities. However, the CA does not consider individuals as detached from their personal and social context, and recognizes that people's actions and choices may depend on other people and on the sociocultural circumstances in which they are immersed (Nussbaum 2007; Sen 1999, 2002: 80–81).

Social elements are seen to have *causal influence*, because they forge circumstances of the individuals' agency and shape their choices and capacities (Bhaskar 1998: 36; Little 1998: 202; Pawson/Tilley 1997: 66; Smith/Seward 2009). A social norm or practice could in fact restrain people's capability sets, or limit one group in favour of another (Robeyns 2006: 369) by influ-

---

2 Furthermore, while arguing in favour of using capabilities rather than commodities to assess people's quality of life, Sen (1990: 70f.) acknowledges that the variability of the social context is one of the elements that make commodities unsuitable for assessing quality of life, because they will affect "the translation of income or commodity into human development outcomes." Related to this, he states that different customs and habits also imply different commodity requirements to attain the same capability (Deneulin/McGregor 2010: 504f.).

encing individuals' reasoning and actions in relation to their position within social structures (Smith/Seward 2009). It has also been acknowledged that the connections between sociocultural norms and welfare institutions have to be investigated carefully in this respect (Olson 2002: 381), because the structure and the policies issued by welfare institutions may reflect part of these norms. Sen and Nussbaum observe that people may be keen to produce adaptive responses especially in case of deprivation and suffering, particularly when the hardship is justified by social or cultural practices and related to hierarchy and domination (Nussbaum 1996: 32; Sen 2002). The relation between a good or a service and the capability set is seen as mediated by three groups of *individual conversion factors* (Robeyns 2005: 99), namely personal, social, and environmental. They help explain the definition of the capability set given a spectrum of goods and services, and, consequently, the achieved functionings as well. Personal conversion factors, such as physical conditions or various skills, mould the individual conversion from a commodity to a functioning, whereas social conversion factors – public policies, social norms, past and present circumstances – and environmental conversion factors are crucial societal aspects that may affect the translation of goods and services into functionings (Robeyns 2003, 2005). Especially the social and the environmental conversion factors play a connective role between the social context and the capability set, and make it possible to account for a number of societal attributes (Robeyns 2006). It is therefore paramount to bear them in mind when analysing and assessing policies.

2.2 Social context and the definition of the capability set

If, for Amartya Sen, capabilities are real opportunities, for Martha Nussbaum, they also include abilities, skills, and powers. She implies that conversion factors are included in the concept of capability itself (Robeyns 2003: 75) and distinguishes three categories of capabilities. *Basic capabilities* are innate abilities such as sensory and speech abilities. *Internal capabilities* are more mature states of a person that enable her or him to exercise a specific capability if the circumstances and constraints permit. Some of these capabilities do not require undertaking specific actions to be developed, but only a lack of obstacles. For example, if well-nourished, a person becomes sexually mature simply by growing. Other capabilities need the favourable support of the surrounding environment, such as, in the case of Kosovo, developing certain attitudes towards different communities. But from a certain point, these capabilities are available, potentially ready to be used. Finally, *combined capabilities* are the internal capabilities together with the (favourable) external conditions that effectively enable the person to exercise them (Nussbaum 2000: 83ff., 2011: 20f.). A person can develop a general stereotype-free attitude towards a certain community (internal capability), but she or he may be hindered by the surrounding system of social and cultural norms. The distinction between internal and combined capabilities may sometimes be blurred, because, in some cases, benign circumstances would suffice to develop internal capabilities whereas, in other cases, practicing them is crucial.

Similarly, Des Gasper (1997, 2002) distinguishes analytically between *O-capabilities* (*O* for *option* and *opportunities*) and *S-capabilities* (*S* stands for *skill* and *substantive*). The first corresponds roughly to Sen's focal concept of capability and Nussbaum's internal capabilities, the latter to Nussbaum's combined capabilities. O-capabilities – the set of existing options that one could embrace – take into account constraints and opportunities related to not only individual power but also particular social, cultural, political, and economic settings (Gasper 2002: 447; Otto/Ziegler 2006). They are therefore closely linked to and shaped by the social context in which they are embedded. S-capabilities have been defined as the "space of capacities, skills, and attitudes" (Otto/Ziegler 2006: 272), and are connected at the empirical level with the O-capabilities. It is possible to recognize in these differentiations how the context plays a major role in defining capabilities at the analytical and evaluative level, because it helps to forge them. In fact, social and cultural arrangements may, on the one side, shape the set of options available to one person and, on the other side, influence people's attitudes and mindsets in respect to them (Sen 1993).

2.3 Social context and public discussions over capabilities

The sociocultural context is also recognized as crucial for the definition of the capability set in another way in both Sen's and Nussbaum's approaches (Robeyns 2006). Despite substantial differences in the way they define the capability set, they both ideally grant power of negotiation to citizens. Sen does not endorse a specific list of capabilities, but emphasizes that relevant capabilities have to be established through public discussions and democratic procedures (Sen 1999, 2002). He argues that such means can help to achieve a better message about the role and value of capabilities (Sen 2004), and stresses the role of democratic institutions, civil rights, and a free press in the creation of social norms, ethics, and goals (Hill 2003: 119). Nussbaum (2000, 2003), in contrast, introduces a concrete list of ten universal capabilities, but stresses nonetheless that the list has been elaborated while having cultural pluralism in mind. As a consequence, it is open-ended and needs to be further adjusted at a local level on the basis of the specific history and cultures (Nussbaum 2007: 314). She also maintains that the list could be used by the population as a basis for negotiations with governments (Nussbaum 2003, 2007).

However, despite being recognized as influential for the definition of the capability set, the social context and its components are not analysed in depth within the CA. This may lead to a rather general and blurred framework when it comes to evaluating and assessing policies. Being able to frame the context and analyse it in depth is therefore essential if we are to gain a better understanding of the circumstances that can allow capabilities to flourish or, in contrast, to be hindered.

3 Power in the Capability Approach

Connected to the social context, power relations also tend to be overlooked within the CA framework. Although Sen does recognize that power dynamics internal to households may lead to different command over and access to resources and ultimately to inequalities, generally, issues of power are quite disregarded (Deneulin/McGregor 2010: 502f.), particularly the "role of institutionalized power in causing or perpetuating inequalities in individual opportunities to achieve" (Hill 2003: 117). Feminist economics acknowledge the connection between people's social relations and structured institutions and their capabilities to live the life they have reason to value; however, unless some light is shed on power relations, analysis of well-being and attempts to enhance human capabilities will be unsuccessful (Hill 2003: 117).[3] Social power is a complex concept encompassing social, cultural, psychological, and economic dimensions, all necessary to understand relations among social groups and between groups and institutions (Hill 2003: 120). It is exercised mainly through institutions and social practices (Fraser 1989), and some researchers, such as Bagchi (2000), argue that a closer look at institutions would help to point out abuses of monopoly and power. Also, Pettit maintains that the results of capability-driven policies run by state institutions should be the "absence of domination" (Pettit 2001: 18), meaning that policies should broaden citizens' choices and substantive freedoms, and not support intergroup prevalence. Hamilton (1999: 545) follows a similar direction when noting that the expansion of freedom has "political consequences for institutions and for the distribution of normative power". He also recognizes that the CA does not identify declared preferences within individuals' interests, but analyses people's capability to achieve valuable functionings from different perspectives, taking into consideration a variety of additional infor-

---

3 Despite the CA being an individualistic theory, Sen notes that some general inequalities may be better assessed when analysed in terms of groups and intergroup relations (Sen 1992: 101, 117; Hill 2003).

mation.[4] Among these perspectives, public discourses and social structures are definitely relevant aspects, because they contribute to shaping (avowed) interests and capabilities. Some may in fact cause a mismatch between substantive freedoms and declared interests; and, to reverse this, we need to create new knowledge and shift paradigms, and this, in turn, would trigger resistance from those whose authority is diminished (Hill 2003: 123). Power has also been associated with shared knowledge and understanding (Lukes 1974)[5] – which include cultural, social, and economic capital – that enable the functioning of a given society and its institutions (Haugaard 1997). Shifts in the knowledge paradigm and in discourses happen regularly, and they support the change in social practices and social structures that determines the active "regime of truth production" (Hill 2003: 127) by dominant groups.

Therefore, it seems possible to argue that within the CA, there is a great need to further deepen not only the – also methodological – analysis of social context and structures but also the issue of power relations. The first will seemingly allow a better understanding and evaluation of the creation of the capability set, of the process that leads from the social contexts to the conversion factors, and of the public debates that could foster the development of a society and the broadening of citizens' capabilities. The second would encourage the understanding of some of the mechanisms that regulate the shaping of sociocultural structures and practices.

4   Discourse and education policy formation in Kosovo

In order to strengthen the analysis of context and power relations, it is decisive to focus on language and discourse. Their importance has been acknowledged increasingly in modern social processes, especially those related to the emergence of the *knowledge-based economy* or *semiotic economies* (Luke 2002). Fairclough (2003) talks about discourse-driven social change in which "language, text, and discourse become the principal mode of social relations, civic and political life, economic behaviour and activity, where means of production and modes of information become intertwined in analytically complex ways" (Luke 2002: 98). For this reason, Critical Discourse Analysis (CDA) has become especially valuable in policy analysis, because, on the one side, it encourages investigation of the relation between language and other

---

4   Hamilton (1999) demonstrates that Sen's version of the CA integrates a theory of true interest, used to scrutinize people's admitted interests with additional information (such as conversion factors, context, etc.), in order to produce internal and external evaluations of them.
5   Lukes (1974) claims in fact that the knowledge that feeds the decision making embodies a dimension of power.

social practices (e.g. events and texts) and, on the other side, unveils power relations (Taylor 2004: 433). CDA is also remarkable because it is openly critical, concerned with revealing power relations along with their political consequences, and committed to progressive social change (Fairclough 2003). Critical instances in policy analysis are also highlighted by Louise White (1994), who claims that policy analysis should draw upon CDA together with reflections on political values and the critical assumptions embedded in any policy.

The concept of discourse contributes to understanding policy formation (Ball 1990), because it helps to explain the configuration of power and knowledge that policy statements conceal (Foucault 1981). In policy documents, the language actually serves a political purpose, contributing to the construction of public consent over a certain topic, hiding potential social conflicts, and producing particular meanings and signs (Codd 1988: 237). As part of the political negotiation process (Ingram et al. 2007), words included in policy are carefully selected and revised according to opposite interests that shape it. The language of policy is therefore linked to political compromises and power relations (Kemmis 1990) as well as to particular social groups, and policies can be defined as "the exercise of political power" (Codd 1988: 325) – and language is used to legitimize the process (Codd 1988: 325). The basic task of policy analysis is therefore to track ideological, economic, and political changes and how they affect the dynamics of policy debate and policy formulation (Ball 1990). Bassler (2005: 6) depicts particularly how politics and education are inseparably connected in South Eastern Europe, showing that reforms cannot be implemented without political support, no matter how much national or donor investment is provided. Changes at all levels of education are very often politically driven, making the analysis of the social and cultural context – and of related power relations – very relevant, allowing events and texts to be placed within a fitting framework. Education policies are in fact considered to be a matter of "authoritative allocation of values" (Kogan 1975: 55; Prunty 1985: 136) that cannot be independent from the social context. Policy statements in fact provide a blueprint of an ideal society and ultimately define the cultural norms that count in education (Ball 1990; Taylor 1997). Their formation originates in ideological layers (Shapiro 1980: 328) endorsed by different actors. Donald (1979: 100) argues that "implicit in the question of the restructuring of education, then, is the question of how the state exercises and imposes its power in part through the production of the *truth* and *knowledge* about education." *Truth* and *knowledge* cannot be separated from issues of power and interests, but they also do not respond to dominant interests alone. Analysing continuities and discontinuities in transitional settings (Bîrzea 1994) as well as in sociohistorical contexts is therefore utterly decisive, because the relevance of the past and its influence on the present is also emphasized locally (Bîrzea 1994; Sommers/Buckland 2004: 24).

In this view, Kosovo constitutes a fascinating case study, due to the complexity of the transformation processes it is enduring. In the last decades it has been subjected to a permutation of status – which is still under discussion – of its general ideological setting and of its administrative apparatus. Moreover, it is involved in a process of conflict resolution and peacebuilding. Kosovo was in fact a province of former socialist Yugoslavia, and after the disintegration of the federation remained under the Republic of Serbia. Between the end of 1980s and the beginning of the 1990s, Serbian authorities revoked Kosovo's autonomous status – including that in education – leading to the establishment of a system of parallel structures – including schools, universities, hospitals, and so forth – self-managed and funded by the Kosovo Albanian community including the diaspora. This, linked to the first self-declaration of independence in 1991,[6] was the first attempt to show that the Kosovo Albanian community was capable of self-government. After the conflict in 1999, the structure was formally dismantled, and its institutions substituted by the Joint Interim Administrative Structure (JIAS) established by the UNMIK with the aim of performing basic administrative functions and promoting the establishment of substantial autonomy and self-government in Kosovo. The international administration managed a gradual return of power and competencies to the newly established local institutions, but concurrently, the Serbian administration kept functioning in Serbian-majority enclaves and districts. Education in Kosovo is therefore connected to a high degree of emotionality, especially in the way different communities view and relate to educational changes (Sommers/Buckland 2004: 23). It has been a controversial issue for a long time, and one of the main fields in which ethnic unrest and autonomy claims are being played out (Kostovicova 2005). Both major ethnic groups, Albanians and Serbs, had an ethnically exclusivist approach to education, to the extent that "the Serbian–Albanian battle over education has been battle for Kosovo in miniature" (Kostovicova 1999: 12). All these transformations entail shifts in power and renewal of actors, and consequently continuous adjustments in the education system. At the same time, after the end of the conflict, dozens of international organizations flocked to the territory of Kosovo, each of them trying to pursue their own agenda, creating a sort of "laboratory for blueprint of societies and statebuilding intervention" (Daxner/Riese 2011: 24) There was neither a shared concrete implementation plan nor an effective coordination mechanism. This fact, together with struggles between different actors and the changeability of the situation, slowed down progress in education and other fields. Moreover, in a few years, Koso-

---

6 The self-declared Kosovo parliament initially declared Kosovo a republic in Yugoslavia and then an independent country on 22 September 1991. Ibrahim Rugova was elected president in May 1992.

vo went from being considered a post-conflict and post-emergence territory to being canalized in the EU accession path (Daxner/Riese 2011: 26) with these perspectives still overlapping. This may create tensions between the actors involved, and it is visible in different stakeholders' and local institutions' discourses on education that focus, in some cases, more on human rights, multi-ethnicity, and peacebuilding (Krasniqi 2010); in other cases, more on standards, quality improvement, and knowledge economy, thereby showing a progressive Europeanization and technologization of discourses. It is also possible to notice gaps in coherence between discourses produced by and for either local or international actors.

5 Social context and power relations in Critical Discourse Analysis

Such tensions and discontinuities leave their mark in policy documents and can emerge through an analysis of their language and discourses. Connections between analysis of language and development policy were already drawn by Des Gasper (1996, 2000), one of the most active scholars in the CA. He has suggested that Discourse Analysis (DA) can make a valuable contribution to the analysis of development policy. Although he does not seem to be very concerned with the critical aspect of the analysis, power relations, and so forth – which are, in contrast, major issued in CDA – he does point out that DA pays great attention to texts and their contexts (Apthorpe/Gasper 1996) that both ought to be contrasted in policy analyses. In his view, texts should be analysed intensively and minutely as mirrors of some specific perspectives and contexts. His starting point is policy analysis rather than DA, and the aspects to be analysed are similarly mainly linguistic (e.g. keywords, stylistics devices) and extra-linguistic (e.g. argumentation, problem framing, narratives, and rules of validation) (Apthorpe/Gasper 1996: 6).

As defined by Norman Fairclough, CDA draws on a concept of language as an essential element of all social processes – such as an education system (Williams 1977) – and consists of the "analysis of the relationships between discourse and other elements of social practices" (Fairclough 2003: 205). The entry points for CDA are social concerns and social problems, aiming primarily at disclosing what is said and can be said in a given society together with the techniques that mark and bound discourse limits (Wodak/Meyer 2009: 36). CDA, as the name suggests, takes a critical stance and is concerned especially with the shifting role of discourse within the profound global changes of contemporary society (Chouliaraki/Fairclough 1999; Fairclough 1993, 2003) along with the way in which language is central to the formation of subjugation and inequality (Rogers et al. 2005: 368). On one hand, in fact, it aims to unfold how semiosis may lead to the creation and reproduction of unequal power relations (dominance, exclusion, marginalization) and ideologies, and how, in more general terms, it influences human *well-being* (Fairclough 2009: 163). On the other hand, it intends to show the ways in which dominant discourses are challenged and reversed, and the chances to address the social *wrong* and ultimately improve human well-being. Interestingly one of the most powerful forms of oppression is assumed to be internalized hegemony, a form that includes both coercion and consent (Rogers et al. 2005: 368). However, it has to be noted that despite referring to human well-being and social wrongs, in contrast with the CA, CDA does not provide a normative concept of well-being – except in a negative way as absence of unequal power relations. Moreover neither it departs from a collective idea, nor does it try to reach some conclusions on individual well-being. Concerning this, CA could in turn integrate CDA, by providing a clearer definition of the research issues and purpose for the analysis.

CDA is based on the concept that social practices, defined as "stabilized forms of social activities" (Fairclough 2003: 205), are structured in different social elements, dialectically related (Fairclough 2003: 205):

a. Activities
b. Subjects and their social relations
c. Instruments
d. Objects
e. Time and place
f. Form of consciousness
g. Values
h. Discourse/Semiosis

The same practice may in fact be represented from different positions and angles: for instance the teaching of history in Kosovo is generally conceived by local actors as a nation-building tool, and this is very apparent especially in school textbooks. When they relate to international donors though, such as in project reports, they tend to embrace their agenda, according to which history is more connected to the discourse on human rights and the protection of minorities. All aspects forming a social practice have to be analysed in CDA together with the language in order to gain a fuller understanding of the research field. What can be defined as context therefore becomes substantial in the analysis. Applied to policy analysis, CDA leads to a profound understanding of the circumstances of the production, distribution, and consumption of a policy along with the social practices in which texts are immersed. At the same time, it frames the power relations between a policy's producers and consumers. The context is to be considered at three levels: local, related to those events that are object of analysis; institutional, including the social and political institutions that frame the local context; and societal, that is, the larger governing bodies, including policy programs and historical circumstances that influence the local and international context (Rogers 2004: 238). Education policy is therefore better understood when immersed in its threefold context, and the process of issuing the document is considered from both a political and a historical perspective (Nelles 2005). This can ultimately provide information on and help to assess the context in which the capability set is generated. Specifically in the case of Kosovo, some main contextual lenses to be considered are the national historical background (including the Yugoslavian past), the parallel system, the collective memory of recent and past conflicts, and the structure of Kosovan families and society including the diaspora. Also, it is very relevant to bear in mind the political scene, both internal, such as political parties' relations and rural–urban contrasts; and international, such as the general European enlargement process and donors' agendas.

Different discourses are connected to the different perspectives people have on the world, and these depend on their positions, their relationships, and their social and cultural identity. Relationships between people are also influenced by the discourses they are variously associated with. It is easy to see how positioning themselves inside a particular discourse and social practice would give people a certain perspective and eventually influence the way they (re)act and interact within it. This links up with the social conversion factors mentioned in the previous paragraph. In the case of education in Kosovo, discourses related to past circumstances, or to some current policy, and the way people position themselves within them, may in fact influence their capability set – for instance, their perceived and actual chances to interact with members of different communities. It also seems possible that a certain discourse may lead to contrasting outcomes in different settings: for instance, the acquisition of a rather nationalistic discourse in a Kosovo-Albanian history textbook is appreciated in a different way in a nationalistic or more multicultural setting, and could influence people's (perceived) capability set. CDA is especially effective because it considers many aspects that go beyond single texts; views them as being embedded in given social, political, historical and spatial circumstances; and analyses the dialectical connections between them. For this reason, articulation of the context becomes very crucial in the analysis.

Discourses include a representation of the way things are, but also of how things potentially could or should be (Fairclough 2003) and in which direction change ought to happen. That means they give an image of possible social practices and social orders – including social relations, activities, actors, and so forth (Harvey 1996) that may eventually be enacted and realized on both a material and semiotic level (Fairclough 2003: 207). Discourses are not mere ideology, but forge and actualize social reality (Jäger/Maier 2009: 36). As Fairclough implies, public policies therefore delineate how we act and the rules we must abide by; public policies are in fact one of the instruments through which we are socialized regarding what is thinkable and unthinkable (Bernstein 1996).

Albeit it is quite easy to point out the mere existence of power in policymaking, it is more challenging to show how the power is generated, the role that some individuals play, and the implications that the powers have on recipients. In Kosovo, the struggle between local authorities and international stakeholders is visible in most of the educational policy discourse. On one side, through the support of the international community – also financial – the Kosovo government gains legitimacy in front of not only other countries but also the local population. On the other side, however, it has to comply with other countries' directions and discourses in order to retain and increase their support, and therefore continues to be somehow dependent on foreign assistance (Narten 2010). But international actors also have an interest in operating in Kosovo, driven as they are by various reasons be they political, such as improving the stability of the country and ultimately the whole region, or financial, such as ensuring the continuity of their programmes. Therefore the power struggle goes in both directions, creating a sort of *asymmetric interdependence* (Bache/Taylor 2003).

Power is a central concept in CDA, drawing mainly on Foucault's idea of power as a systemic and constitutive element of society (Foucault 1996: 324). Language conveys and reveals power (Fairclough 1989/1991) and texts are rarely considered as the product of a single person, but rather as the result of a negotiation of different discourses led by power relations embedded in certain discourses and genres. They show traces of contrasted discourses and ideologies competing for dominance and are therefore a site of struggle for dominance. Power relations are observable *in* discourse and *behind* discourse. The first refers to moments in texts in which power relations are enacted; the second to power-shaped orders of discourse by power participants who control the contribution of less powerful groups (Fairclough 1989/1991). This is achieved in more than one way through constraints in the content, in the social relations established in the text, and in the positions people can take (Fairclough 1989/1991). Fairclough considers ideologies as a stabilized construction of practices that contribute to establishing and reproducing relations of power, domination and exploitation. Particular ideologies may become *hegemonic* and therefore part of the legitimated common sense and more difficult to contest. Nonetheless, he recognizes that one of the unknown issues in the dialectic of discourse is how people may get to *own* a discourse, to position themselves within it and act accordingly. This process, referred to as *inculcation* (Fairclough 2003; Wodak/Meyer 2009), may affect the way people picture and interpret themselves and their activities as well as others. These representations eventually produce new imaginaries, in a sort of circular but not inevitable process. CDA is therefore not only a retrospective analysis, but also an "analysis of the ongoing production of reality through discourse" (Jäger/Maier 2009: 37).

6 Conclusions

Although the CA does recognize the importance of the social context when analysing social policies, it rarely explains how the social context has to be taken into consideration. Methodologically, it tackles neither social context nor power relations. This may well jeopardize the analysis of capabilities by missing out some crucial elements – as we have seen in the case of education in post-war Kosovo. Therefore, it seems that CDA is very valuable for understanding the developments of education policy in Kosovo, because it engages in the social *wrongs* and aims to understand how semiosis ultimately influences human well-being. It also deals in depth with the context in which a policy is immersed, and unveils the framework of power relations that is so crucial in policy analysis. Thus, CDA could support CA both in the analysis of the social context when assessing the creation of the capability set through policy analysis and in the comprehension of the power relations that can affect individual freedom and choices and how they shift over time. CDA moreover provides methodologies of analysis, as well as a critical stance that aims at reversing social inequalities and promoting change. Vice versa, CA could be integrated in CDA by providing normative concepts of well-being and inequality that could help CDA by refocusing the selection of research issues and research objectives and, at the same time, concentrating more on the individual level and on how the social context and power relation may affect it.

References

Apthorpe, Raymond/Gasper, Des (1996): Introduction: Discourse Analysis and Policy Discourse. In: The European Journal of Development Research, 8, 1, pp. 1–15.
Bache, Ian/Taylor, Andrew (2003): The Politics of Policy Resistance: Reconstructing Higher Education in Kosovo. In: Journal of Public Policy, 23, 3, pp. 279–300.
Bagchi, Amiya (2000): Freedom and Development as End of Alienation? In: Economic and Political Weekly of India, 35, 50, pp. 4408–4420.
Ball, Stephen (1990): Politics and Policy Making in Education. London: Routledge.

Barlett, Brendan/Power, Des/Blatch, Peter (2004): Education in a Recovering Nation: Renewing Special Education in Kosovo. In: Exceptional Children, 70, 4, pp. 485–495.

Bassler, Terrice (ed.) (2005): Learning to change: The experience of transforming education in South East Europe. Budapest: Central European University Press.

Bernstein, Basil (1996): Pedagogy symbolic control and identity: Theory, research, critique. Bristol, PA: Taylor & Francis.

Bhaskar, Roy (1998): The Possibility of Naturalism: A Philosophical Critique of the Contemporary Human Sciences. London: Routledge.

Bîrzea, César (1994): Educational policies of the countries in transition. A secondary education for Europe. Strasbourg: Council of Europe Press.

Chouliaraki, Lilie/Fairclough, Norman (1999): Discourse in the Late Modernity: Re-Thinking Critical Discourse Analysis. Edinburgh: Edinburgh University Press.

Codd, John A. (1988): The construction and deconstruction of educational policy documents. In: Journal of Educational Policy, 33, pp. 235–247.

Daxner, Michael/Riese, Sarah. (2011). Long-time Effects from Kosovo, Little Ado About Bosnia-Herzegovina. In: Sicherheit und Frieden, 1, 24–30.

Deneulin, Séverine/McGregor Allister J. (2010): The capability approach and the politics of a social conception of well-being. In: European Journal of Social Theory, 13, pp. 501–519.

Donald, James (1979): Green paper: noise of crisis. In: Screen Education, 30, pp. 13–49.

Fairclough, Norman (1989/1991): Language and Power. London: Longman.

Fairclough, Norman (1993): Critical Discourse Analysis and the Commodification of the Public Discourse. In: Discourse and Society, 4, 2, pp. 133–168.

Fairclough, Norman (2003): Analysing discourse: Textual analysis for social research. London: Routledge.

Fairclough, Norman (2009): A Dialectical-relational approach to critical discourse analysis. In: Wodak, Ruth/Meyer, Michael (eds.) (2009): Methods of Critical Discourse Analysis. London: Sage, pp. 162–186.

Foucault, Michel (1981): The order of discourse. In: Young, Robert (ed.): Untying the text: a post-structural anthology. Boston: Routledge & Kegan Paul, pp. 48–78.

Foucault, Michel (1996): What is Critique? In: Schmidt, James (ed.): What is Enlightenment? Eighteenth-century Answers and Twentieth-century Questions. Berkeley: University of California Press, pp. 382–298.

Fraser, Nancy (1989): Unruly Practices. Minneapolis, MN: University of Minnesota Press.

Gasper, Des (1996): Analysing Policy Arguments. In: European Journal of Development Research, 8, 1, pp. 36–62.

Gasper, Des (1997): Sen's capability approach and Nussbaum's capabilities ethics. In: Journal of International Development, 9, 2, pp. 281–302.

Gasper, Des (2000): Structures and meanings – a way to introduce argumentation analysis in policy studies education. The Hague: ISS Working Paper 317.

Gasper, Des (2002): Is Sen's Capability Approach an adequate basis for considering human development? In: Review of Political Economy, 14, 4, pp. 435–460.

Hamilton, Lawrence (1999): A Theory of True Interests. In: Government and Opposition, 34, 4, pp. 516–546.

Harvey, David (1996): Justice, Nature and Geography of Difference. Oxford: Blackwell.
Haugaard, Mark (1997): The Constitution of Power. New York: St. Martin's Press.
Hill, Marianne (2003): Development as Empowerment. In: Feminist Economics, 9, 2–3, pp. 117–135.
Ibrahim, Solava (2006): From individual to collective capabilities: the capability approach as a conceptual framework for self-help. In: Journal of Human Development, 7, 3, pp. 397–416.
Ingram, Helen/Schneider, Anne/DeLeon, Peter (2007): Social Construction and Policy Design. In: Sabatier, Paul A. (ed.): Theories of the Policy Process. New York: Westview Press, pp. 93–128.
Jäger, Siegfried/Maier, Florentine (2009): Theoretical and methodological aspects of Foucauldian critical discourse analysis and dispositive analysis. In: Wodak, Ruth/Meyer, Michael (eds.): Methods of Critical Discourse Analysis. London: Sage, pp. 34–61.
Kemmis, Stephen (1990): Curriculum theory and the state in Australia. In: Journal of Curriculum Studies, 22, 4, pp. 392–400.
Kogan, Maurice (1975): Educational Policy Making: a Study of Interest Groups and Parliament. London: George Allen and Unwin.
Kostovicova, Denisa (1999): Albanian Schooling in Kosovo 1992–1998: 'Liberty Imprisoned'. In: Drezov, Kyril/Gokay, Bulent/Kostovicova, Denisa (eds.): Kosovo. Myths, conflict and war. Staffordshire: Keele University, pp. 12–20.
Kostovicova, Denisa (2005): Kosovo: The politics of identity and space. London: Routledge.
Krasniqi, Gëzim (2010): The International Community's Modus Operandi in Postwar Bosnia and Herzegovina and Kosovo: A Critical Assessment. In: Südosteuropa, 58, 4, pp. 520–541.
Little, Daniel (1998): Microfoundations, Method, and Causation: Essays in the Philosophy of the Social Sciences. New Brunswick, NJ: Transaction Publishers.
Luke, Allan (2002): Beyond Science and Ideology Critique: Developments in Critical Discourse Analysis. In: Annual Review of Applied Linguistics, 22, pp. 96–110.
Lukes, Steven (1974): Power: A Radical View. London: Macmillan.
Narten, Jens (2010): Dilemmas of promoting 'local ownership': the case of postwar Kosovo. In: Paris, Sisk (ed.): The Dilemmas of Statebuilding. Confronting the contradictions of postwar peace operations. London: Routledge, pp. 252–284.
Nelles, Wayne (2005): Education, underdevelopment, unnecessary war and human security in Kosovo/Kosova. In: International Journal of Educational Development, 25, 1, pp. 69–84.
Nussbaum, Martha (1996): Compassion: The Basic Social Emotion. In: Social Philosophy and Policy, 13, 1, pp. 27–58.
Nussbaum, Martha (2000): Women and Human Development: The Capability Approach. Cambridge: Cambridge University Press.
Nussbaum, Martha (2003): Capabilities as Fundamental entitlements: Sen and Social Justice. In: Feminist Economics, 9, 2–3, pp. 33–59.
Nussbaum, Martha (2007): Frontiers of justice: Disability, nationality, species membership. In: The Tanner lectures on human values. Cambridge (MA): Belknap Press of Harvard University Press.

Nussbaum, Martha (2011): Creating capabilities: The human development approach. Cambridge (MA): Belknap Press of Harvard University Press.
Olson, Kevin (2002): Recognizing Gender, Redistributing Labor. In: Social Politics, 9, pp. 380–410.
Otto, Hans-Uwe/Ziegler, Holger (2006): Capabilities and Education. In: Social Work and Society, 4, 2, pp. 269–286.
Pawson, Ray/Tilley, Nick (1997): Realistic Evaluation. London: SAGE Publications.
Pettit, Philip (2001): Symposium on Amartya Sen's Philosophy. "Capability and Freedom: A Defence of Sen". In: Economics and Philosophy, 17, 1, pp. 1–20.
Prunty, John (1985): Signposts for a Critical Educational Policy Analysis. In: Australian Journal of Education, 29, 2, pp. 133–140.
Robeyns, Ingrid (2003): Sen's Capability Approach and Gender Inequality: selecting relevant Capabilities. In: Feminist Economics, 9, 2–3, pp. 61–92.
Robeyns, Ingrid (2005): The Capability Approach: a theoretical survey. In: Journal of Human Development, 6, 1, pp. 93–117.
Robeyns, Ingrid (2006): The Capability Approach in Practice. In: The Journal of Political Philosophy, 14, 3, pp. 351–376.
Rogers, Rebecca (2004): Setting an Agenda for Critical Discourse Analysis. In: Rogers, Rebecca (ed.): An Introduction to Critical Discourse Analysis in Education. Mahwah, NJ: L. Erlbaum Associates.
Rogers, Rebecca/Malancharuvil-Berkes, Elisabeth/Mosley, Melissa/Hui, Diane/Joseph, Glynis (2005): Critical Discourse Analysis in Education: A Review of the Literature. In: Review of Educational Research, 75, 3, pp. 365–416.
Sen, Amartya (1980): Equality of what? In: McMurrin, Scott (ed.): The Tanner Lectures on Human Values. Vol. 1. Cambridge: Cambridge University Press.
Sen, Amartya (1984): Resources, values and development. Cambridge, MA: Harvard Univ. Press.
Sen, Amartya (1992): Inequality Re-examined. Oxford: Claredon Press.
Sen, Amartya (1993): Capability and Well-Being. In: Nussbaum, Martha C./Sen, Amartya (eds.): The Quality of Life. Oxford: Claredon Press, pp. 30–53.
Sen, Amartya (1999): Development as Freedom. New York: Knopf.
Sen, Amartya (2002): Response to Commentaries. In: Studies in Comparative International Development, 37, 2, pp. 78–86.
Sen, Amartya (2004): Capabilities, Lists, and Public Reason: Continuing the Conversation. In: Feminist Economics, 10, 3, pp. 77–80.
Shapiro, H. Svi (1980): Society, ideology and the reform of special education: A study in the limits of educational change. In: Summer Educational Theory, 30, 3, pp. 211–223.
Smith, Matthew/Seward, Carolina (2009): The Relational Ontology of Amartya Sen's Capability Approach: Incorporating Social and Individual Causes. In: Journal of Human Development and Capabilities, 10, 2, pp. 213–235.
Sommers, Marc/Buckland, Peter (2004): Parallel worlds. Rebuilding the education system in Kosovo. Paris: IIEP.
Sommers, Marc/Buckland, Peter (2005): Negotiating Kosovo's educational minefield. In: Forced Migration Review, 22, pp. 38–39.
Stewart, Frances/Deneulin, Séverine (2002): Amartya Sen's contribution to development thinking. In: Studies in Comparative International Development, 37, 2, pp. 61–70.

Taylor, Sandra (2004): Researching Educational Policy and Change in "New Times": using Critical Discourse Analysis. In: Journal of Education Policy, 19, 4, pp. 433–451.

Taylor, Sandra (1997): Educational policy and the politics of change. London: Routledge.

Walker, Melanie (2003): Framing Social Justice In Education: What Does The 'Capabilities' Approach Offer? In: British Journal of Educational Studies, 51, 2, pp. 168–187.

White, Louise (1994): Policy Analysis as Discourse. In: Journal of Policy Analysis and Management, 13, 3, pp. 506–525.

Williams, Raymond (1977): Marxism and Literature. Oxford: Oxford University Press.

Wodak, Ruth (2008): Introduction: discourse, text, and context. In: Wodak Ruth/Krzyżanowski, Michal (eds.): Qualitative discourse analysis in the social sciences. Basingstoke: Palgrave, pp. 1–29.

Wodak, Ruth/Meyer, Michael (eds.) (2009): Methods of Critical Discourse Analysis London: Sage (first edition published in 2001).

Anika Duveneck

The Contribution of Critical Materialist Theory to Capability Research: Empirical Insights From the Field of Local Educational Politics

1   The CA-adequate concept of communal landscapes of education and its difficult practice

In recent years, German politics reveal a strong trend towards localizing education. More specifically, the concept of "Communal Landscapes of Education" (CLE) is becoming more and more widespread. Extensive programs such as "Local learning" (Lernen vor Ort) from the German Ministry of Education or the federal "Regional Networks of Education North Rhine-Westphalia" (Regionale Bildungsnetzwerke NRW) have been initiated since 2009 in order to foster the development of models for local educational politics. One of the driving forces behind the reorganization of education on a local scale is the assumption that the structures of the German educational system are inappropriate because, as the PISA studies have so often revealed, they produce rather than reduce social inequality.

In contrast to other western welfare states, the German system is characterized by a specific separation of education and public care (Gottschall 2001). Only schooling belongs to the realm of educational politics; whereas childcare, preschool education, and youth work belong to social politics. The special German path is rooted in the historical development of public care during the 19th century that was dominated by the assumption that childcare and childrearing are the responsibility of the family or, more specifically, of mothers. The state's function was reduced to intervention only when the family could not fulfil its role, for example, when working-class mothers had to work in order to contribute to breadwinning. This division of responsibilities led to the implementation of the subsidiary principle for childcare, preschool education, and youth work, and these became the concern of municipal child protective services (Gottschall 2001: 12f.). Further, as the provision of public infrastructure and services is a general concern of municipalities within the national state (Häußermann et al. 2008: 279; Harvey 1989; Schipper 2013: 101f.), they are also responsible for school buildings and education-related domains such as culture and sport – each administered in separate departments. Nonetheless, education in the sense of schooling has always been a state concern. With regard to the division of responsibilities, the system of half-day schooling became dominant so that in the afternoon, mothers would be responsible for their children.

Concerning school, another German specificity is the strong stratification within the three-tier school system to structure access to the labour market. In line with the "take-off-phase" (Gottschall 2001: 14) of industrialization and welfare state development in the late 19th century, the lower track provided a suitable standardized qualification for the industrial sector whereas the upper tracks served as a recruitment qualification for the administration of state bureaucracy.

The basic structures of the German system, meaning the division of responsibilities for public care, school buildings, and other education-related public services on a municipal scale and the organization of schooling by the federal states (representing the state in the federal state), have been maintained up to the present day. Nonetheless, since the crisis of the welfare state in the 1970s (Hirsch 1996: 84ff; Schipper 2013: 103ff.; Lipietz 1985: 125ff.), the social structures have changed considerably.

With regard to the uneven social development as a consequence of the erosion of welfare structures, the half-day system became a problem, because the strong role of the families leads to the reproduction of social inequality: Whereas parents with a high SES can afford to pursue their educational aspirations by paying for extra educational services such as music lessons for their children, parents with a low SES cannot (Duveneck 2012: 9).

The organization of a coherent but diverse system of education and care on a local scale is now discussed as a promising approach to overcome social selectivity and make education a key to social justice (e.g. Bleckmann/Schmidt 2012). Highlighting two core ideas of CLEs, the next section describes some progressive features of the concept that have resulted in it having hardly any opponents but a high degree of affirmation (Reutlinger 2011: 21; Luthe 2008: 337).

- One of its conceptual ideas is to finally make stronger use of the social potential of informal, non-selective education. Hence, by installing structures to systematically include domains such as early childcare, youth work, culture, sports, and so forth, CLEs pursue a *broad understanding of education* beyond the formal and selective school system.
- Further, another means is to provide better education to socially deprived children and youth through a *participative organization of education* based on structures that not only overcome the institutional separation on a local scale but also allow local educationalists to contribute their specific knowledge to the young people's individual needs.

This chapter uses the concept of CLE as an example to discuss the analytical scope of the Capability Approach (CA) and present arguments in favour of an alliance with Critical Materialist Theory. First, it highlights the strong correspondence between the concept of CLEs and the core ideas of the CA. Then, based on an empirical study of a CLE, it presents findings on the relation between the conceptual goals and their realization. This is followed by confronting the analytical contribution of the CA to the emerging distortion between the conceptual goals and their realization with the explanatory potential of Critical Materialist Theory. By identifying the influence of political economy, which deeply shapes the realization of the CLE concept but cannot be detected nor explained by means of CA thereby leading to misleading approaches to public politics, the chapter closes by calling for an alliance of CA with Critical Materialist Theory.

1.1 Correspondence of CLE to the CA notion of educational politics

On a conceptual level, CLEs correspond to the notion of education in the CA. Sen and Nussbaum developed this normative framework to identify economistic constrictions in current public politics and accuse them of severely disrespecting "the complexity of human needs and striving" (Nussbaum 2011: ixf.) and therefore, at least in Nussbaum's version, of violating human dignity (Nussbaum 2011: 161). Insisting that "individuals, and only individuals, are the units of moral concern" (Robeyns 2005: 107f.), the CA conceptualizes an alternative approach to public politics as a means to reach ends such as increased well-being or justice (Robeyns 2005: 95).

The variety of educational opportunities included in CLEs corresponds to the "sensitivity of the capabilities approach to human heterogeneity" (McCowan 2011: 294). Thus, it makes it possible to provide the broad range of distinguishable options that a CA-adequate notion of education demands (Oelkers et al. 2008: 87f.).

Aside from the quantitative aspect of broadening the range of educational options, in qualitative terms, the integration of informal education beyond formal education in schools matches the CA call for education "beyond the notion of human capital" (Sen 1997; cited in Robeyns 2006: 74). From a CA perspective, increasing the relevance of informal education and thereby, offering a more flexible, non-selective educational infrastructure can be considered as an institutional precondition for an education that aims at the development of the full human being (Nussbaum 2003). Further, the concept's claim to adjust educational politics towards young people as "full human beings" (Schubert 2008: 22) instead of reducing them to pupils corresponds to the CA's general call to acknowledge human life in its complexity. The concept's capacity for a CA-adequate reform of educational politics that enables people "to do and to be what they have reason to value" (Sen 2001: 14f.) has become highlighted and discussed in research literature (Bollweg/Otto 2010; Berse 2009: 66ff.) because it opens up a discussion on institutional structures appropriate to unfold the non-economic, intrinsic role that education comprises (Robeyns 2006: 74). Current public politics instead push young people into politically desirable lifestyles.

The idea of a participatory organization of local education also corresponds to the CA. Implementing a new mode of communication between bottom-up and top-down structures makes it possible to open up political structures for participation, so that "sensitivity to the context", which, following Nussbaum (2011: 157), "good education requires", can be considered appropriately. By involving the actors concerned systematically in the organization of local education, educational politics can develop during the course of the process instead of being defined in advance (Bonvin 2009: 17). Correspondingly, the concept promises to realize the CA's understanding of public politics as a means to reach individual well-being. Basically, the consistent use of participatory structures implies no less than the perspective of stopping the instrumentalization of young people by public politics for economic growth, in this case, by narrowing education to the production of human capital.

In a nutshell, there are remarkable overlaps on the conceptual level between the CLE's core conceptual goals and the CA. Accordingly, the concept is an appropriate example to discuss the CA's analytical scope and limitations.

1.2 Empirical findings: Actual realization of CLE in a district of Berlin

The empirical findings to be discussed here in order to reveal the CA's analytical contribution are derived from an empirical case study on local educational politics that asks about the impact of political-economic conditions of interurban competition on the concept's realization in practice.

The research case is a local educational project in a socially deprived, multicultural district in Berlin. In 2006, the district became a nationwide synonym for the failure of the school system, school violence, and failed integration after teachers at a local secondary school wrote a public letter highlighting the tremendous problems within the school due to segregation and underfunding. In response to this scandal, in 2008, the mayor presented a concept to make the school (which had since been converted into a comprehensive school) part of a social-integrative local educational project in cooperation with various educational actors, namely, early childcare centres, a youth club, the public health service for children and youth, vocational promotion, the municipal school for music, and the community college. The project claims to provide better education for the young people by merging the single educational actors into one comprehensive "campus".

With regard to the variety of included institutions and their potentials, the concept pursues a broad understanding of education that goes beyond school. A local network based on the conceptual goal of participatory organization has been established to implement this merger into a common project on the practical level. The process is supported by two heads of the project who have been employed by the municipality.

In order to develop appropriate administrative structures and thereby develop a pioneer model for local educational politics, the district authority set up a new steering committee to overcome the given structural separation. This was composed of involved representatives from the district, service providers, the federal school administration, and foundations. Additionally, a new "campus administration" was established for the formal, comprehensive administration of the included institutions. Depending on the particular administrative status of the single institutions within the given system, the administration's legal influence differs in each case: The campus administration, for example, has the right to administer the youth club. By drawing up the contracts with service providers, it can exert a strong influence here; whereas in other cases such as the child and youth health service, the school authority can only agree on informal cooperation. With regard to the conceptual goals and the establishment of an administrative model for the organization of education on local scale, the case fulfils the criteria for an empirical study of CLEs.

The study is based on 15 expert interviews conducted between March and May 2012 with actors involved in the project. These included the head of the school, the head of a childcare centre, the head of the youth club, the provider of school social work, and representatives of vocational training and the child and youth health service. Using an explorative guideline, the interviews asked respondents about their experiences in the project and the effects on their educational work. Based on these descriptions, later analyses discussed the relation between the conceptual goals of this CLE and its realization in practice in the context of the political-economic conditions shaping local politics in order to reconstruct their influence. To contextualize the findings, additional interviews have been conducted with the heads of the local educational project, the administrator, representatives of local educational networks, and an involved parents initiative.

1.2.1 Empirical findings on the realization of the broad understanding of education in practice

The realization of the broad understanding of education in practice is illustrated by presenting statements by three educational actors located along the dimension of formal to informal education.

School: The head of the school shows a positive attitude towards the local educational project. She confirms the structures of the (school-centred) project to be supportive: "It creates opportunities" (Head of the school).

With regard to the district's new administration, she stresses that the school is not affected by changes at all. This is not surprising, because the new administration is recruited from the former department for the school. The only change is that the administration moved to the school building, which is rather an advantage because of better opportunities for informal communication. The professional supervision of the school remains the responsibility of the federal senate, so, in this concern, there are no changes either.

Childcare service: The head of the childcare service is also satisfied, especially because as part of the project, she feels her work is finally being appreciated, which was not the case before. Due to the fact that independently from the local educational project, childcare centres are obliged in any case to increase cooperation with (and the children's transition to) school these days, she considers the project to be an "environment in which current reforms in early childcare are esteemed" (Head of early childcare). The informal collaboration within the local educational network provides a lot of support the obligatory contact with the school.

Further, as concluding contracts with the municipality is a matter of the childcare centre's service provider and not of the institution itself, the head does not notice administrative changes. She only mentions discussions concerning changes in responsibilities that, at this point, do not affect the childcare centre.

Youth club: The youth club is an institution of informal education that, despite always having had intermittent cooperations with the school, benefits from its general autonomy, because this allows it to provide alternative learning opportunities that are independent from the school. This is especially important for socially deprived children and youth: the target group of the concept that is structurally discriminated by the selective formal school system.

For the heads of the project, it turned out that being part of the project has only a negative impact on their work: In the end, they felt forced to end their engagement for professional reasons, because they did not feel that their informal work was being appreciated within the local actors' network by the district authority, and that they were structurally reduced to a "servant of the school" (head of the youth club).

In this case, especially the district's impact was considered to be destructive. In the context of the project, administration of the youth club has been shifted from the youth department to the school department. This shift had a serious impact on professional work: According to the head of the youth club, the former relations to the youth department were highly productive, based on trust and freedom. This relation was sacrificed in the context of the project and its common administration. Although the school authority is not adequately qualified for this task, it now draws up the contracts with the providers of the youth club and therefore, has the power to define what youth work has to fulfil. As a consequence, youth work is obliged to give up its crucial autonomy in order to support the schools in, for example, technical and scientific education and thereby loses its particular potential for socially deprived young people.

In sum, the interview data provide evidence that the local educational project is structured to the effect that the educational institutions involved support the school more systematically. For the school itself and institutions that have to increase their cooperation with schools in any case (such as childcare centres), the local educational project provides a supportive frame. However, by making other institutions support the formal educational success, it lowers the recognition of informal education as an autonomous educational approach. In contrast, rather than broadening the understanding of education, it seems to increase the focus on formal education.

1.2.2 Empirical findings on the realization of participative organization of education

A general result of the empirical study that applies to all the educational actors included is that none of them receive financial support for their contribution to the project. As one of its main goals is to provide good education despite the underfunding of educational institutions, for example, by cooperating with each other or acquiring and coordinating external funds, a lot of additional work arises in the context of the project. Further, as taking personal responsibility for the educational success of the young people is defined as consensus within the project, extra efforts without extra pay seem to be expected of them morally. With regard to the corresponding workload, a serious overload was mentioned in almost every interview.

Further, according to the interviews, the attempts at self-organization developed by the actors involved in the local network were repelled by the district. Accordingly, their extra efforts and willingness to give parts of their autonomy to the common project are not compensated by any contribution of their specific knowledge to the official decision-making in local educational politics that would deliver the promised context-sensitive and individual organization of education in line with the concept's claim for participatory organization of education.

Hence, in practice, participation means a one-sided exploitation of the local actors' resources to compensate the public underfunding of education rather than the establishment of a new mode of communication between top-down and bottom-up structures.

1.2.3 Conclusion

In conclusion, with regard to narrowing education to formal education rather than realizing a broader understanding of education and with regard to the one-sided exploitation of the involved actors rather than realizing a participatory organization of education, the interview data reveal that the relation between the concept of local educational politics and its realization in practice is characterized by distortion.

1.3 Analytical contribution of the CA to the distorted relation from concept to practice

I shall now discuss the analytical contribution of the CA to the empirical findings and then, its analytical limits. So what does the CA contribute to the distortion of the concept's progressive conceptual goals in practice?

First, the CA integrates the fact that an adequate concept is not enough, but systematically requires an adequate realization in practice in its conceptual framework. In their definition of a CA concept of education, for example, Oelkers et al. (2008: 87f.) explicitly stress that opportunities on a rhetorical level do not count. They count only if they are "effectively realizable" to provide people with the capability to live the life they have reason to value. So from a capabilities perspective, the realization of the analysed CLE in Berlin would be evaluated as inadequate, and it would call for a better realization. However, explaining why the concept is not realized in practice goes beyond the scope of the normative framework, and it is construed to define to what extent the current conditions of public politics allow its realization.

This brings us to the fact that the CA systematically takes into account that the realization of its notions on public politics necessarily requires appropriate conditions.

With regard to participation, Bonvin (2009: 19f.) defines preconditions that have to be fulfilled in order to realize the CA notion. He points out that all involved actors have to be equipped with resources that allow them to defend and enforce their position; additionally, there has to be an absence of predefined goals derived from cost–benefit analyses, competitive politics, or other external sources. Otherwise, politics do not allow an adequate realization from a CA perspective.

As a normative framework to conceptualize and evaluate public politics, the contribution of applying the CA is to detect and highlight the economic constriction occurring in the realization of public policies such as CLE. With regard to the realization, it provides a moral underpinning to the accusation that neither the range of educational opportunities nor the organization of education can be understood as adequate to the complexity of human life and striving. With Nussbaum's version, the practical realization revealed by the empirical findings can even be accused of violating human dignity (Nussbaum). Particularly with regard to the moral impetus of the project mentioned before, it offers strong arguments for the actors involved to insist on a realization according to the (CA-adequate) concept.

Moreover, CA research also links identified restrictions to the broader political context: The economic narrowing of education to the production of human capital can thus be considered in the context of the broader modernization of welfare state structures (Oelkers et al. 2008: 85). Capabilities research on new localism takes into consideration that a main target of current politics is to compensate a lack of public funds by activating civil society. So Bonvin (2009: 19f.) anticipates the empirically detected gap between the broadening of the local actors' influence on a rhetorical scale although their actual influence is limited. But although CA researchers state these conditions and blame them for being inappropriate, the CA neither focuses on them explicitly nor can it explain why or how they cause economic restriction.

This brings us to the analytical limits of the CA. Because, as Robeyns (2005: 94) stresses, it is explicitly not a theory, explaining goes beyond its scope. This requires the addition of explanatory theories. In order to be accessible for a broad range of fields, research interests, and research questions, the CA is strategically equipped with an "open-ended and underspecified nature" (Robeyns 2011: no page) so that it can be combined with a broad range of theories.

2 Understanding the distortion from concept to practice from a Critical Materialist perspective

To gain an adequate understanding of the relation between the concept of the empirical case in Berlin and its realization in practice, I add Critical Materialist Theory because it relates the empirical findings to the current conditions that shape politics in general and local educational politics in particular.

2.1 The Perspective of Critical Materialist Theory

The theoretical perspective of Critical Materialism focuses explicitly on the fundamental conditions of society that other theories simply take for granted (Heinrich 2005: 60). Based on Marx's analysis of capitalist societies (Marx 1968), it assumes that under conditions of capitalism, social reality inevitably becomes shaped by the logic of political economy. Hence, an adequate understanding of social matters in general (such as the realization of local educational politics) cannot be isolated from this logic, but has to take it into account.

The major analytical insight of materialist theory is that in capitalist societies, social reality is dominated by the abstract rule of capital. That is, society is shaped to fulfil capital's need to produce surplus value rather than to fulfil the needs of its members. In other words, the capitalist mode of social production does not serve people's needs but instrumentalizes them for (and subordinates them under) the logic of capital that strives for surplus alone (Marx 1970: 649). In his reconstructive analysis of society in capitalism, Marx revealed the social nature of the systemic production of economic constriction that materializes in practice but, due to mechanisms of naturalization and "fetishization", occurs "behind the backs" (Marx 1968: 14) of the actors.

Hence, the general task of materialist theory is to take materialized social practice as a starting point – that is why it is called "Materialism" – and to reveal the relation to political economy via reconstruction and theoretical reflection (Dahme/Wohlfahrt 2012: 159). Based on its analytical potential to explain economic constriction in social life in relation to the conditions of capitalism, materialist theory is conceptualized as an instrument to disclose the subordination of people and to empower them to strive to create conditions that allow them to fulfil their needs and attain well-being (Heinrich 2008: 75). It is important to stress the emancipatory impetus that particularly characterizes *Critical* Materialism, the version of materialist theory that has been developed by Critical Theory of the Frankfurt School in distinction to historical or dialectical materialism: The latter has been used as official doctrine of Marxism–Leninism and still has a broad influence on the public reception of materialist and Marxist theory (Schmidt Noerr 1991: 16f.).

2.2 Reconstruction of political-economic influence on CLE

From the perspective of Critical Materialist Theory, the task is to find out whether and to what extent the relation between the conceptual goals of CLE (broad understanding and participative organization of education) and their realization in practice (formalization of education and one-sided exploitation) can be explained by the political-economic conditions that currently shape local politics.

To make the political-economic processes visible that shape the realization of the concept in practice "behind the backs of the actors", they have to be identified via reconstruction. To provide the theoretical backdrop for this purpose, based on materialist research literature on local politics, the next section outlines features of local educational politics under current political-economic conditions. By then discussing whether these features can explain the relation from concept to practice, the influence can be reconstructed theoretically.

There is consensus among materialist geographers that, in the last decades, as a consequence of the reduction of financial funding and redistributive mechanisms by the national state, municipalities are situated within an interurban competition (Harvey 1989; Brenner 2004; Heeg/Rosol 2007; Schipper 2013; Häußermann et al. 2008). Under these conditions, they have to act entrepreneurially. Through being urged to create financial growth to stay (or become) competitive, they have to compete for high performers such as enterprises or middle-class families. Further, municipalities have to invest economically. Due to financial austerity, they are obliged to reduce their public expenses as much as possible (Häußermann et al. 2008: 248) – particularly for those who are socially deprived and obliged to act under conditions of permanent underfunding.

The question is: can the distorted relation between the conceptual goals of the local educational project and its actual realization described by the actors concerned be traced back to these political-economic conditions that shape local politics?

2.2.1 Broad understanding of education in concept – Stronger focus on school in practice

Hence, the first question that has to be discussed is whether the relation between the conceptual goal of the broad understanding of education and the stronger focus on institutions supporting the formal school system can be explained with reference to interurban competition.

In this respect, it is important to mention the increased importance of school for middle-class parents' choice of their place of residence. This has been identified in various studies on urban sociology (Atkinson 2006; Ball 2003; Bunar 2010; Butler/Robson 2003; Butler 2012; Maloutas 2007; Noreisch 2007; Reaveaud/Zanten 2007). Within this trend, local educational politics becomes a promising means for municipalities to attract this target group and thereby, raise their competitiveness. With regard to the high proportion of socially deprived inhabitants and the image loss caused by the scandal in 2006, the district in the empirical study is not attractive to the majority of middle-class parents but only to "alternative" middle-class parents. With regard to research on gentrification (e.g. Smith 1987; Hamnett 1991; Lees et al. 2010), the presence of this group called "pioneers" raises the attraction for middle-class parents in general, and thereby induces a process of social upgrading. Accordingly, it is to be assumed that in this case, alternative middle-class parents are the target group.

So can the distortion of the broad understanding of education be traced back to the orientation towards the preferences of the target group for entrepreneurial local politics? The analysis shows that indeed, the research case meets the preferences of alternative parents for education that are characterized by a specific contradictoriness (Cucciara/Horvat 2009: 986).

On the one hand, alternative middle-class parents distinguish themselves through their political striving for educational justice (Merkle et al. 2008: 201). Whereas other parents might avoid schools in multicultural, socially mixed neighbourhoods, alternative parents are especially interested in this kind of school (Cucchiara/Horvat 2009: 975; Reay et al. 2007: 1042). In the interview, the representative of the local parents initiative states:

> I don't want to be someone who only demands the best for her own child – otherwise, I probably wouldn't live here. What I want is a good sense of togetherness, that one can learn from each other and find common resources. I'm not eager to have the best class teacher; I simply don't like this attitude. (representative of parents initiative)

In this sense, the research case highly matches their preferences. First, due to the media attention the school attracted in 2006, it attained high prominence as a diverse, multicultural school. Further, the projects' social-integrative claim and its inclusion of various educational institutions correspond to the target group's interest in alternative, progressive types of schools.

On the other hand, alternative middle-class parents also do not want to sacrifice their children for their political convictions. Hence, the schools still have to match a certain level of middle-class expectations (Cucciara/Horvat 2009: 986). The representative of the parents initiative states:

> I'm glad that my daughter is not the only German in her class, that there are other German children in school, of course, so that there are other ones on her level. (The contradictory character is revealed when she immediately adds: "But I want to have a good mix. I want the school to stay multicultural." (representative of parents initiative)

By involving the parents initiative systematically in the local planning and networking process, by considering their wishes and meeting their expectations, the local district structurally makes sure that it is in contact with the preferences of organized local parents. So the representative of the parents' initiative reports in the interview that they feel highly welcome within the project. Furthermore, the strong orientation towards the parents' preferences is expressed by their privileged consideration in the project:

> Basically, we really have a lot of possibilities. Let's see what's happening, but they will approach us if there is anything to arrange. It's not bad to have the option to influence the project. (representative of parents initiative)

For example, the district agreed to meet the parents' demand to build a new parent centre as an integral part of the project.

Corresponding to the target group's particular contradictory preferences, the project successfully allows combining a multicultural school with an orientation towards middle-class expectations. This is confirmed empirically in the following reference:

> I'm totally happy to have this project. I think it really is a good school, directly within the neighbourhood: Great! (representative of parents initiative)

In sum, the fact that the actual realization of the local educational project does not lead to a broader understanding of education but strengthens formal institutions such as schools and childcare centres can be attributed to the desire to attract the target group. Hence, there is strong evidence that the realization is shaped by the political-economic logic of interurban competition.

2.2.2 Participative organization of education in concept – one-sided exploitation in practice

The second aspect refers to the relation between the conceptual goal of the participative organization of education and the one-sided exploitation of the involved educational actors in practice.

In this regard, it is important to consider that financial austerity is forcing socially deprived municipalities to reduce public funding. As a consequence, in this situation of underfunding, there are no capacities for extra funding beyond their duties. Instead, there is a strong demand for cost-neutral policy models such as local educational politics that make use of the resources provided voluntarily by involved actors. The activation of the resources of local actors and civil society to compensate public underfunding by appealing to their moral responsibility as in this research case has been recognized as a strategy to realize lean politics (Häußermann et al. 2008: 202; see also Mayer 2003). This, therefore, explains the district's interest in the participatory structures.

The fact that the local actors do not receive more influence on decision making in the form of a participative organization of education in turn for compensating public deficits can also be attributed to local politics under conditions of austerity.

As Peck (2012) demonstrates, austerity limits the scope of political decision making to entrepreneurial politics for competitive advantages. With reference to factual financial constraints, political alternatives that do not follow this imperative but other premises are immediately declared to be unaffordable and therefore, not realizable. Because the local actors' striving for a context-sensitive organization of education is oriented towards the actual local needs but not towards competitiveness, there is no space for its realization in any case. On that base, their participation in official decision making does not make any sense. Hence, there is evidence that in this aspect as well, the realization of local educational politics is shaped by the political-economic conditions of interurban competition.

2.2.3 Conclusion

The findings show that, at least within the scope of the methodological accessibility through reconstructive identification, there is evidence that the realization of the educational policy is shaped by the logic of the political economy: Taking the materialized practices as a starting point, it turns out that the realization does not follow the conceptual goals that correspond highly to the CA. Instead, because the political-economic conditions of interurban competition urge the district to act entrepreneurially and competitively, they become instrumentalized for this imposed purpose.

3 Implication of the empirical findings for the CA

With regard to the CA, it is important to stress the fact that as long as concepts such as CLE are realized under conditions of capitalism, structural reasons inevitably lead to the distortion of progressive goals.

As long as conditions of competition urge municipalities to force processes of social upgrading, realizing projects in favour of socially deprived inhabitants contradicts their structural interests. Instead, the conditions of interurban competition mobilize municipalities to use the potential of local educational politics to attract target groups with a higher social status that will enhance their competiveness. Hence, socially deprived children and youth are finally means and not ends, because they are instrumentalized by the district to meet alternative middle-class parent's preferences for socially mixed schools. These parents, on the other hand, are a means to stabilize the ongoing process of social upgrading. Finally, because, under current conditions, municipalities are well advised to force competitive processes of gentrification, in practice, the local educational project does not reduce social inequality but causes a new dimension of disadvantage for those who are said to be supported.

As long as municipalities are urged to reduce public funds by austerity (and additionally do not have capacities for politics that do not serve competitiveness anyway), they are well advised to use the local actors' unpaid efforts to compensate the public underfunding and support socially deprived children and youth in order to fulfil their entrepreneurial and competitive goal of realizing a cost-neutral, location policy that will attract middle-class families. However, at the end of the day, it can be seen that the participative organization of local education does not lead to a more context-sensitive and need-oriented education, but to the systematic compensation of underfunding to the cost of local actors within the narrow frame of competitive politics under conditions of austerity.

What the example of CLE should demonstrate is that to gain an adequate understanding of the realization of public politics (such as local educational politics), the structural conditions and political economic logics of capitalist societies inevitably have to be taken into account. Analyses that disregard the political-economic processes working behind the backs of the actors in capitalism but deeply shaping social reality miss the crucial point. Accordingly, conclusions drawn on this incomplete analysis tend to be misleading.

Further, the contribution of Critical Materialist Theory to the realization of the CA-adequate educational agenda is to point to the fact that adequate conditions are required that (1) do not let politics instrumentalize education for competitiveness but allow it to serve the individual interests of people rather than competition, and (2) allow local actors to follow their sense of responsibility without becoming instrumentalized to compensate systematically for the reduction in public spending.

The analysis is used as example to show empirically that the logics of political economy place actors (such as municipalities) in capitalist societies structurally in opposition to progressive conceptual claims that could very well correspond to the CA. With regard to the CA, it means that as long as its proponents do not systematically take into consideration that the conditions of capitalism are highly influential but fundamentally contradictory to its normative claims for individual well-being and social justice, the CA's approaches to public politics are constrained within capitalist reality. Hence, an adequate analytical understanding of social reality under conditions of capitalism is vital for the realization of the CA's agenda in practice.

Critical Materialist Theory has the explanatory potential to make the fundamental contradictions visible. Further, it shows that overcoming or at least challenging capitalist conditions is the precondition to reach well-being and justice consistently. Finally, it shares the CA's emancipatory impetus to make people's well-being an end rather than subordinating it under economic logics. So in conclusion, the CA is well advised to strike up an alliance with Critical Materialist Theory.

References

Atkinson, Rowland (2006) Padding the Bunker: Strategies of Middle-class Disaffiliation and Colonisation in the City. In: Urban Studies, 43, 4, pp. 819–832.
Ball, Stephen. J. (2003) Class strategies and the education market: The middle classes and social advantage. London: Routledge Falmer
Berse, Christoph (2009): Mehrdimensionale Bildung im Kontext kommunaler Bildungslandschaften. Bestandsaufnahme und Perspektiven. Opladen: Budrich Uni-Press.
Bollweg, Petra/Otto, Hans-Uwe (eds.) (2011): Räume flexibler Bildung. Bildungslandschaft in der Diskussion. Wiesbaden: VS Verlag.
Bonvin, Jean-Michel (2009): Der Capability Ansatz und sein Beitrag für die Analyse gegenwärtiger Sozialpolitik. In: Soziale Passagen, 1, pp. 8–22.
Bleckmann, Peter/Schmidt, Volker (eds.) (2012): Bildungslandschaften. Mehr Chancen für alle. Wiesbaden: VS Verlag.
Brenner, Neil (2004): New state spaces. Urban governance and the rescaling of statehood. Oxford: Oxford University Press.
Bunar, Nihad. (2010). Choosing for quality or inequality: Current perspectives on the implementation of school choice policy in Sweden. In: Journal of education policy, 25, 1, pp. 1–18.
Butler, Tim (2012) Gentrification in London – Modes of middle class establishment in a Global City. In: Herrmann, Heike/Keller, Carsten/Neef, Rainer/Ruhne, Renate (eds): Die Besonderheit des Städtischen. Entwicklungslinien der Stadt(soziologie). Wiesbaden: VS Verlag, pp. 265–284.
Butler, Tim/Robson, Garry (2003). London Calling: The Middle Class and the Remaking of Inner London. Oxford: Berg.
Cucchiara, Maria Bloomfield/Horvat, Erin McNamara (2009): Perils and Promises: Middle-class Parental Involvement in Urban Schools. In: American Educational Research Journal, 46, 4, pp. 974–1004.
Dahme, Heinz-Jürgen/Wohlfahrt, Norbert (2012): Ungleich gerecht? Kritik moderner Gerechtigkeitsdiskurse und ihrer theoretischen Grundlagen. Hamburg: VSA Verlag.
Duveneck, Anika (2012): Kommunen übernehmen Verantwortung für gute Bildung. In: Kommunale Bildungslandschaften. Schriftenreihe zu Bildung und Kultur, 9. Berlin: Heinrich-Böll-Stiftung.
Gottschall, Karin (2001): Erziehung und Bildung im deutschen Sozialstaat. Stärken, Schwächen und Reformbedarfe im europäischen Vergleich. ZeS-Arbeitspapier, 9, Bremen (unpublished).

Hamnett, Chris (1991). The Blind Men and the Elephant: The Explanation of Gentrification. In: Transactions of the Institute of British Geographers, 16, 2, pp. 173–89.
Harvey, David (1989): From Managerialism to Entrepreneurialism. The Transformation in Urban Governance in Late Capitalism. In: Geografiska Annaler, 71, 1, pp. 3–17.
Häußermann, Hartmut/Läpple, Dieter/Siebel, Walter (2008): Stadtpolitik. Frankfurt am Main: Suhrkamp.
Heeg, Susanne/Rosol, Marit (2007): Neoliberale Stadtpolitik im globalen Kontext – Ein Überblick. In: Prokla. Zeitschrift für kritische Sozialwissenschaft, 149, 37, 4, pp. 491–509.
Heinrich, Michael (2005): Kritik der politischen Ökonomie. Eine Einführung. Stuttgart: Schmetterling-Verlag.
Hirsch, Joachim (1996): Der Nationale Wettbewerbsstaat. Staat, Demokratie und Politik im globalen Kapitalismus. Berlin, Amsterdam: Edition ID-Archiv.
Lees, Loretta/Slater, Tom/Wyly, Elvin K. (2010): The gentrification reader. London, New York: Routledge.
Lipietz, Alain (1985): Akkumulation, Krisen und Auswege aus der Krise: Einige methodische Überlegungen zum Begriff ‚Regulation'. In: Prokla. Zeitschrift für kritische Sozialwissenschaft, 15, 1, pp. 109–137.
Luthe, Ernst-Wilhelm (2009): Kommunale Bildungslandschaften. Rechtliche und organisatorische Grundlagen. Berlin: Erich Schmidt Verlag.
Maloutas, Thomas (2007). Middle class education strategies and residential segregation in Athens. In: Journal of Education Policy, 22, 1, pp. 49–68.
Marx, Karl (1970): Critique of the Gotha Program. In: MEW 3. Moscow: Progress Publishers, pp. 13–30.
Marx, Karl (1968): Das Kapital. Kritik der Politischen Ökonomie. In: MEW 23. Berlin: Dietz.
Mayer, Margit (2003): Das Potenzial des Regulationsansatzes für die Analyse städtischer Entwicklungen am Beispiel territorialer Anti-Armutspolitik. In: Brand, Ulrich/Raza, Werner (eds.): Fit für den Postfordismus? Theoretisch-politische Perspektiven des Regulationsansatzes. Münster: Verlag Westfälisches Dampfboot, pp. 265–280.
McCowan, Tristan (2011): Human rights, capabilities and the normative basis of "Education for All". In: Theory and Research in Education 9 ,3, pp. 283–298.
Merkle, Tanja/Henry-Huthmacher, Christine/Wippermann, Carsten (2008): Eltern unter Druck. Selbstverständnisse, Befindlichkeiten und Bedürfnisse von Eltern in verschiedenen Lebenswelten. Stuttgart: Lucius & Lucius.
Noreisch, Kathleen (2007a): School Catchment Area Evasion: The Case of Berlin, Germany. In: Journal of Education Policy, 22, 1, pp. 69–90.
Nussbaum, Martha Craven (2003) 'Women's education: A global challenge'. In: Signs 29, 2, pp. 325–55.
Nussbaum, Martha Craven (2011): Creating capabilities. The human development approach. Cambridge, Mass: Belknap Press of Harvard University Press.
Oelkers, Nina/Otto, Hans-Uwe/Ziegler, Holger (2008): Handlungsbefähigung und Wohlergehen: Der Capabilities-Ansatz als alternatives Fundament der Bildungs- und Wohlfahrtsforschung. In: Otto, Hans-Uwe/Ziegler, Holger (eds.): Capabili-

ties. Handlungsbefähigung und Verwirklichungschancen in der Erziehungswissenschaft. Wiesbaden: VS Verlag, pp. 85–89.
Peck, Jamie (2012): Austerity urbanism. American cities under extreme economy. In: City, 16, 6, pp. 626–655.
Raveaud, Maroussia/Zanten, Agnes van (2007). Choosing the local school: middle class parents' values and social and ethnic mix in London and Paris. In: Journal of Education Policy, 22, 1, pp. 107–124.
Reay, Diane; Crozier, Gill and James, David (2011) White Middle Class Identities and Urban Schooling. Hampshire: Palgrave Macmillan.
Reutlinger, Christian (2011): Bildungsorte, Bildungsräume und Bildungslandschaften im Spiegel von Ungleichheit. Kritischer Blick auf das "Räumeln" im Bildungsdiskurs. In: Petra Bollweg/Hans-Uwe Otto (eds.): Räume flexibler Bildung. Bildungslandschaft in der Diskussion. Wiesbaden: VS Verlag, pp. 51–69 .
Robeyns, Ingrid (2005): The Capability Approach: a theoretical survey. In: Journal of Human Development, 6, 1, pp. 93–114.
Robeyns, Ingrid (2006): Three models of education: rights, capabilities and human capital. In: Theory and Research in Education, 4, 1, pp. 69–84.
Robeyns, Ingrid (2011): The Capability Approach. In: Zalta, Edward N.: The Stanford Encyclopedia of Philosophy. http://plato.stanford.edu/archives/sum2011/entries/capability-approach/ (13.03.2014).
Schipper, Sebastian (2013): Genealogie und Gegenwart der "unternehmerischen" Stadt. Neoliberales Regieren in Frankfurt am Main 1960–2010. Münster: Verlag Westfälisches Dampfboot.
Schmidt Noerr, Gunzelin (1991): Für einen kritischen Materialismus der Praxis. In: Schmidt Noerr, Gunzelin/Lutz-Bachmann, Matthias (eds.): Kritischer Materialismus. Zur Diskussion eines Materialismus der Praxis. Für Alfred Schmidt zum 60. Geburtstag, pp. 11–48.
Schubert, Herbert (2008): Netzwerkkooperation – Organisation und Koordination von professionellen Vernetzungen. In: Schubert, Herbert: Netzwerkmanagement. Koordination von professionellen Vernetzungen – Grundlagen und Praxisbeispiele. Wiesbaden: VS Verlag, pp. 7–105.
Sen, Amartya (1997): Editorial: Human capital and human capability. In: World Development, 25, 12, pp. 1959–1961.
Sen, Amartya (2001): Development as freedom. Oxford, New York: Oxford University Press.
Smith, Neil (1987): Gentrification and the Rent Gap. In: Annals of the Association of American Geographers, 77, 3, pp. 462–465.

Education and the Capability Approach

Joshua Eshuchi

Human Capital, Capabilities and Education Quality in Kenya

1 Introduction

The Education for All (EFA) campaign has increased children's access to and participation in education and many countries are now on course to achieve universal primary education (UPE). However, increases in enrolment have led to a corresponding decline in education quality attributable to a lack of or an inequitable distribution of resources. Moreover, completion rates in primary schooling are still low in many countries due to both entrenched inequalities and the knock-on effects of increased enrolments thus undercutting education's role in human development (UNESCO 2012). A further complication arises from the broad spectrum of conceptualizations of what constitutes education quality engendered by the wide range of different political and cultural discourses. In the Kenyan context, quality is enmeshed in historical and socio-economic issues arising from the post-colonial heritage of the education system and its entrenched socio-cultural inequalities. These have a pervasive impact on the quality of education by structuring learners' educational experiences and outcomes (Ojiambo 2009). Furthermore, the issue of education quality is furthermore mired in a morass of conflicting discourses that come into play due to the influence on educational policy and practice of the World Bank and other multilateral development organizations. The human capital approach has been dominant in the education sector, mostly influenced by neoliberal theories of economic growth through investment in human capital. However, the human development approach is gradually becoming influential in international development due to its focus on rights and social justice (Tikly 2010).

A robust framework for education quality should be guided by explicit values that engage with the cross-cutting issues underpinning education, the most pertinent being effectiveness, efficiency, equity, relevance and sustainability (Barrett et al. 2006). Such a framework should also generate four types of proxy indicators convergent with the measurement of the outcomes of a quality education. Input indicators reflect the supply of educational resources; access indicators identify socio-economic, cultural and geographical conversion factors that facilitate access to educational resources, output indicators identify the impact of provision of educational resources to a population; and, finally, outcome indicators identify the impact of educational policy and practice in achieving development (Vos 1996: 3). An analysis of the historical and socio-economic context should also inform the framework with regards to inequalities in schooling and the relevance of the education provided to the particular needs of learners and their communities. In particular, the framework should focus on teaching and learning processes and how these influence learners' participation and outcomes, because standardized summative tests belie the differences in learners' experiences and do not provide valid data on quality. And lastly, the framework should be self-reflective and critical of education's role in development (Tao 2010).

This chapter engages with two theories prominent in the conceptualization and measurement of education quality, namely the human capital approach and the Capability Approach (CA). It first discusses education quality as conceptualized from the two perspectives and then presents the inherent features and complexities of Kenyan primary education. The core of the chapter is a comparative discussion of the human capital approach and CA as two competing quality frameworks in the Kenyan education system.

2 Conceptualizing education quality

2.1 The Human Capital Approach and education quality

Human capital formation entails a targeted increase of requisite skills and knowledge through investment in education. This is expected to raise incomes, increase national productivity and foster economic growth. Private and social returns to investment in education are measured with the aim of informing policy on resource allocation and educational inputs (Roemer 1990). Literacy and numeracy are the basic skill set to be acquired in primary education and further developed at higher levels in order to ensure that individuals possess the general and job-specific skills that enable integration into the labor market (Becker 1964). Education quality can be conceptualized as the quantifiable outcomes achieved by individuals after completion of a particular level of education as measured against specified inputs, with conversion rates signifying the efficiency and effectiveness of the schooling system. This instrumental approach to education has been predominant in development policy such as the Structural Adjustment Programs of the World Bank. These neoliberal policies have had undue influence on educational discourse and practice, championing a focus on cost efficiency, standardized testing and marketable skills (Sifuna 1990). Assessment of a country's stock of human capital is necessitated by the government's need to pursue policies that will effectively improve it. This has three conventional forms of measurement; output-, cost-, and income-based approaches. The output-based approach utilizes school enrolment rates, accumulated years of schooling at employment age, average years of schooling and the ratio between skilled adults and total adults as a measure of the stock of human capital. Cost-based approaches on the other hand calculate depreciating costs of investment in an individual's human capital. Finally, income-based approaches focus on returns to individuals from the labor market in the form of incomes relative to their investment in education (Keeley 2007; Psacharopoulos 1995).

Although the human capital approach does not offer an explicit conceptualization of education quality, school effectiveness and efficiency measured by a linear input-output model functions as a proxy measure. Inputs can comprise such components as financial resources, infrastructure, teachers and educational resources. These inputs are processed within the education system to produce outputs relevant to the needs of the economy and job market in the form of skilled individuals. The effectiveness and efficiency of education systems is pursued through market-led approaches influenced by rational choice theory. Favored approaches include; the fostering competition between schools through greater school choice for parents; decentralized management and greater school autonomy to give schools maneuvering room in a competitive education market, and greater accountability achieved through benchmarking and publication of schools' performance data. To assess the effectiveness and efficiency of primary education, resource allocations are measured against standardized test results and transition rates. Even though human capital theory accepts that schooling has positive externalities and social benefits, these are rarely encompassed in any measurement, with most models focusing on private and social rates of return as indicated by increased incomes and economic growth. In a globalizing world, there is greater emphasis on international standardized tests such as PISA, TIMSS, and SACMEQ. There is a limited engagement with inequality in education, with some effort to include disaggregated data based on axes of inequality such as gender, poverty and region (Hanushek/Wößmann 2008; Keeley 2007).

The main shortcoming of the human capital approach is the linear input-output relationship that ignores inter-related and multidirectional relationships between various factors in schooling. This input-output orientation posits schools as black boxes, because standardized tests rarely consider the learners' experiences and their impact on performance. Moreover, standardized tests and input indicators have over time become the rationale of quality rather than proxy indicators. This is evident in cases in which teaching in schools becomes focused on ensuring learners pass exams rather than acquire other equally valuable outcomes on affective, cultural and social dimensions (Appiah/McMahon 2002). The screening effect of human capital approaches, given the focus on satisfying a labor market offering limited opportunities, leaves learners with unsatisfactory grades and no viable alternatives after schooling, because education does not prepare them for livelihoods outside the formal labor market. This is related to the issue of the relevance of education, in which educational content and pedagogy geared towards passing examinations does not necessarily consider the needs and livelihood strategies of learners and their communities (Ojiambo 2009).

2.2 The Capability Approach and education quality

The CA is a normative framework that provides an evaluative space to assess human agency and well-being based on well-being freedom (opportunity to achieve well-being), well-being achievement (extent to which well-being has been achieved), agency freedom (opportunity to pursue goals that one values) and agency achievement (extent to which goals have been achieved). Freedom is measured primarily in terms of capabilities whereas achievements are measured in terms of functionings (Sen 1999). Commodities are resources that can be employed to achieve a range of capabilities or functionings. Functionings on the other hand are the states of beings and doings that people are able to achieve while using the commodities at their disposal. Transformation of commodities into functionings is mediated by socio-economic, environmental, and individual conversion factors. From the CA perspective, education is a process that expands human well-being and agency, requiring the integration of rights and capabilities into educational discourse and practice to ensure that all learners have effective opportunities within and through education. A quality education enables all learners to realize capabilities they require to become economically productive, develop sustainable livelihoods, contribute to democratic societies and enhance wellbeing. The actual required outcomes vary according to context but at the end of the basic education cycle must include threshold levels of literacy, numeracy and life skills. (Tikly 2010: 139)

CA requires a quality framework to address inclusion, relevance, participation and minimum thresholds. Education should be inclusive to ensure universal access and achievement of valuable outcomes, regardless of socio-economic and political inequalities. In particular, schooling should ensure equity in the distribution of inputs to ensure that all learners receive a level appropriate to their needs. The curriculum and pedagogy should be relevant to the needs and livelihoods of society. This requires engagement with processes within schooling and their impact on learners' experiences and subsequent outcomes. The principle of participation requires decision-making processes about quality to be undertaken in consensus with all stakeholders such as the state, parents, teachers, children and civil society to ensure accountability. And lastly, the quality framework should specify a minimum threshold that all learners should achieve, reflecting CA's origins as a partial theory of justice focusing on sufficiency (Tikly 2010; Unterhalter 2003). This is essential in ensuring that all learners receive sufficient opportunities to develop the basic capabilities they need for their future capability development (Nussbaum 2000).

Quality measurement within the CA is based on multidimensional indicators. First, there should be indicators reflecting the context of the education system and the impact of socio-economic and political structures on learners' outcomes. This makes it necessary to consider the implementation gap between policies and practice, the outcomes gap between societal expectations and learners' achievements, and the learning gap between the curriculum and actual learning by investigating learners' experience in their home-school-community interaction (Vaughan 2007). Second, there should be indicators reflecting inputs necessary for the schooling process and their effectiveness in fostering learning and valuable outcomes. Because requisite inputs vary by context, their identification requires close engagement with stakeholders. Pertinent inputs include trained teachers, effective school management, educational material, infrastructure and mitigation of home-based factors such as poor nutrition (Oduru/Bosu 2010). And last, the framework should have indicators that reflect processes within schools and systems. A focus on processes is enhanced by having a system that is built upon democratic debate over the nature of quality, accountability to stakeholders, effective quality assessment mechanisms, a relevant and inclusive curriculum, effective pedagogy, and mitigation of inequality among learners (Tikly 2010).

It is incumbent upon policymakers and stakeholders to identify relevant capabilities to be incorporated in quality frameworks. In basic education, it is fairly easy to select basic capabilities and essential education outcomes such as numeracy, literacy, life skills, and basic scientific knowledge. However, the actual content and pedagogy still depends on their valuation by constituents. Unterhalter (2003) selects capabilities by cross-referencing various components of education with the evaluative aspects of capabilities. This enables an in-depth examination of how socio-economic and political conditions influences agency and well-being in primary schooling.

Table 1: Cross-referencing of capabilities and education

Aspects of capabilities	Aspects of education
Well-being achievement	Completion of primary school and acquisition of essential education outcomes
Well-being freedom	Socio-economic conditions conducive to completion of primary school and acquisition of outcomes
Agency achievement	Aspirations to and choice of valuable education outcomes to pursue in relation to livelihoods, present well-being and future well-being
Agency freedom	Socio-economic conditions conducive to development of reasoning abilities and conceptualizations of a good life

Source: own illustration adapted from Unterhalter 2003: 6

There are various capabilities lists, some closely connected to education that can serve as a starting point (Nussbaum 2000: 78; Vaughan 2007: 119; Tao 2010: 9; Terzi 2007: 37) and Robeyns (2005: 205) provides a methodological guide for justification of list of capabilities. A two-fold classification of capabilities can inform selection of capabilities for children, who are not fully adult and thus not necessarily able to make fully-informed choices in exercise of their agency. In such a classification, primary education develops children's O-capabilities (opportunities) which are essential for later on when children need to develop S-capabilities (skills). This two-fold classification enables a division of capabilities into basic capabilities that provide children with opportunities to participate in basic schooling and higher order capabilities comprising skills that are based upon the basic capabilities (Gasper/Van Staveren 2003).

3 Approaches to quality in Kenyan primary education

3.1 Primary school education in Kenya

Kenya is an East African country with an ethnically diverse population of 40 million and a high incidence of poverty, unemployment and socio-economic inequality. The current 8-4-4 education system, introduced in 1984 as a response to the perceived quality inadequacies of the previous system, consists of eight years of basic education, four years of secondary education and a minimum of four years of higher education. Pupils sit for the Kenya Certificate of Primary Education (KCPE) exams at the end of the eight years of the first cycle. In 1963, the independence government promised free universal education to all to be achieved through a gradual abolition of user fees. However this was rolled back with the introduction of cost-sharing measures in the 1980s. In 2003, in response to global development commitments, the Kenyan government re-introduced free primary education (FPE). This led to increased enrolment given that many children had been denied access due to financial constraints. Currently, Gross Enrolment Ratio[1] in Kenya stands at 113%. However, the survival rate to Grade 5 is relatively low at 81% with a lower transition rate to secondary schooling of 70% (Ojiambo 2009). Clearly, there has been commendable quantitative growth, but when one focuses on the quality of education offered, the picture is bleak due to lack of resources, poor pedagogy, inequalities, political interference, and geographical marginalization. Education funding is not sufficient to cover all input costs such as teachers' salaries, infrastructure, free primary education and textbooks. This has led to a perennial shortage of educational resources and overcrowded classrooms, especially in the wake of massive enrolments due to FPE. Given the overcrowded classrooms, most children learn by rote rather than receiving sufficient individual guidance from teachers. Moreover, most children have not mastered the language of instruction and this creates problems with regards to understanding the content. English and Kiswahili are the official languages, with English designated as the language of instruction in schools. However, teachers and pupils tend to use their native languages and Kiswahili in both the classroom and social situations. The relevance of the curriculum to the realities and livelihoods of the children is limited, given its focus on transitions to higher levels without any connection to the socio-economic conditions of the children's lives and their communities. This is all the more important given that more than one-half of children who complete primary school are unable to go to secondary school due to the lack of enough places or economic restrictions, whereas a primary school certificate does not provide enough qualification to access the labor market (Ministry of Education 2008; Ojiambo 2009).

Socio-economic inequalities also abound in the system, as reflected in the high drop-out rates and low transition rates prevalent in some regions and social groups. Furthermore, education itself plays a role in the exacerbation of these restrictions, especially through socio-cultural reproduction of socio economic status, language and culture. This is evident in differences that arise through urban children having an advantage in English language instruction over rural children who rarely use English out of school, cultural practices among communities such as the Masai that valorize traditional socialization over formal schooling and children from poorer families having consistently lower attainments than middle-class children (Uwezo 2012). Inequalities in and through education are shaped in part by the social structure of education and processes within schooling, leading to social exclusion

---

1   The gross enrollment ratio can be greater than 100% as a result of grade repetition and entry at ages younger or older than the typical age at that grade level.

through delinquency, crime and unemployment. Given that the system is focused only on transitions and outcomes, these contextual problems are rarely addressed by Kenyan education policy and practice. Political interference in education has also contributed to poor quality, because regions out of political favor have regularly been denied funding and expansion of educational opportunities. However, the main issue that has been decried regarding quality has been the exam-based KCPE system. A focus on exams has led to a system in which schools teach learners how to pass exams rather than enabling them to acquire useful competencies. Furthermore, the usefulness of the KCPE exam has been questioned, given that its' functional purpose is to screen learners for admission to secondary school, with those failing to make the transition obtaining no useful skills or recognition from the cycle (Sifuna 1990; Ojiambo 2009).

3.2 Conceptualization and measurement of education quality in Kenya

Due to asymmetrical global power structures, international organizations, and above all the World Bank, have long been able to influence Kenyan education policy. Over the years, both the conceptualization and measurement of quality has been informed by neoliberal best practice and human capital approaches that did not necessarily suit the Kenyan education system. The Structural Adjustment Programs (SAPs) were enforced in many developing countries as a precondition for World Bank aid and whereas some education systems such as Botswana successfully implemented these reforms, countries such as Kenya and Uganda were negatively impacted, leading to lower enrolment and deteriorating quality (Ojiambo 2009). Kenyan educational quality standards are elaborated in the Sessional Paper No. 1 of 2005 and are defined by three variables; enrolment rates, the quality of inputs into the instructional process, and the quality of pupil outcomes as measured in KCPE. Inputs standards are set out in the Handbook for Inspection of Educational Institutions and reflect the input-output orientation of the human capital approach. These standards refer to; school size, pupil-teacher ratio, teacher workload pupil-textbook ratio, pupil-toilet ratio, quality of classroom buildings, and available classroom space (Ngware et al. 2010). Since 1994, Kenya has participated in the Southern and Eastern Africa Consortium for Monitoring Educational Quality (SACMEQ). In cooperation with the International Institute for Educational Planning, this consortium has undertaken research and testing to ensure policymakers have reliable information with regards to planning or education quality. SACMEQ key objectives are; to obtain baseline data for selected inputs in primary schools, to assess conditions of primary schooling in relation to national benchmarks, to inform equitable allocation of educational inputs across primary schools and administrative regions, to measure reading and literacy competencies of learners in Grade 6, and to ascertain which education inputs have most impact upon educational commitments. Regarding the latter, the Education for All Index (EDI) is used to measure progress towards EFA and is a composite of four EFA goals, namely, enrolment ratios, survival rates to Grade 5 (a proxy for quality), adult literacy rates, and gender parity. The goals of early childhood education and life skills are omitted due to the difficulty of measuring them quantitatively (UNESCO 2006). Given the contested nature of these measures in the educational debate in Kenya, there has been a push by academics, civil society and even the Ministry of Education to pursue more comprehensive and relevant measures of education quality that reflect the national goals of Kenya and enable the education system to monitor the true state of learning quality in the nation's schools.

3.3 Uwezo Annual Learning Assessment

The Uwezo Annual Learning Assessment (ALA) was launched in 2009 to ascertain whether education policies and practice lead to outcomes desired by learners and their communities. Uwezo means "capabilities" in Swahili and reflects the grounding of the scheme in the CA. Furthermore, the scheme aims to secure greater accountability within the education system by ensuring that parents and the public are aware of actual levels of children's learning and capability acquisition in literacy and numeracy, thus giving impetus to the national debate on education and putting pressure on the state to improve education quality. Uwezo focuses on home and community factors that impact on children's learning. The scheme was motivated by the lack of tangible improvements in children's learning despite increased investment in education. ALA aims to provide a rigorous, evidence-based approach to improve of education quality through three components; large scale assessment, communication of results to the public and facilitation of national debate on education quality (Uwezo 2012). The 2012 ALA is the most comprehensive assessment of education quality in Kenya and covered all 158 districts in the nation. The household-based Randomized Control Trial tested a total of 180,000 children aged 6-16 years. Tests assessed their competencies in completing arithmetic problems and reading English and Kiswahili at Standard 2 level, which is set as the threshold at which children are expected to have acquired basic literacy and numeracy. In addition, the survey investigated factors that impact upon learning such as government policies; the relation between the native language and literacy in English and Kiswahili, teacher and pupil absenteeism, teacher shortages, community participation in schooling, spatial marginalization, development initiatives, nutrition, and family socio-economic status. The results have consistently revealed the poor quality of learning. Uwezo releases an annual National Assessment Report that is accessible in the public domain to policymakers, practitioners and stakeholders. Uwezo's reports have been instrumental in policy dialogue to inform the new Kenya Education Bill (2012) and in the development of the National Assessment System for Monitoring Learner Achievement (Ministry of Education 2011).

3.4 National Assessment System for Monitoring Learner Achievement

The National Assessment System for Monitoring Learner Achievement (NASMLA) was established by the Ministry of Education in response to stakeholder concerns about the insufficiency of KCPE as a monitoring tool because it does not provide background information about the context in which learning takes place. NASMLA builds upon UNICEF's Monitoring Learning Achievement in Lower Primary (MALP) and aims to introduce regular and systematic monitoring of education outcomes in the Kenyan system. NASMLA has five specific objectives; providing baseline data to inform implementation and reform of educational standards, identifying trends in learner achievements to inform curriculum development, institutionalizing the of monitoring of learner competencies in the education system, delivering reliable and valid data to inform policymaking processes, and identifying inequalities that prevent learners from achieving essential outcomes (Ministry of Education 2008). The first assessment in 2009 investigated major determinants of Standard 3 learners' academic achievements in literacy and numeracy, with a focus on personal, home and school backgrounds. The plan is to carry out a follow-up study when the learners are in Standard 6. The assessment was underpinned by a two-level model of factors hypothesized to influence pupil achievement. Two categories of variables were hypothesized to directly influence achievements at Level 1, namely individual pupil characteristics and the home environment compared to five categories at Level 2, namely, teacher characteristics, classroom environment, school headteacher characteristics, school environment and regional environment (Ministry of Education 2008: 5). The results mirrored the Uwezo reports, indicating that quality of education, in particularly in relation to processes in school, was below par. Level 2 factors played a particularly relevant role in the prevailing low quality, given the poor infrastructure, poor pedagogical cultures in school and regional norms and values detrimental to children's education. Poverty was identified as the major stumbling block towards children's participation in and completion of basic education, given that indirect and opportunity costs of schooling remained a major challenge that interrupted children's learning. The survey recommended various strategies for achieving a quality education such as a focus on learners' participation in schooling processes, better teacher training and professional development, systematic monitoring of learners' achievement and greater involvement of parents and other stakeholders in policy and planning at the Ministry of Education.

4 The Capability Approach and education quality in Kenya

The CA assesses education through its contribution to substantive human freedoms rather than serving a production function. These freedoms are operationalized as capabilities and their associated functionings that can be instrumental (test scores, certification and productivity), intrinsic (agency, autonomy and well-being) and positional (access to social positional goods). IN this approach, educational inputs are effective if they fulfill human needs and aspirations rather than labor market and productivity concerns. This provides a useful value basis for assessing the quality of education. Capabilities offer an alternative metric that encompasses more than mere skills, a distinction with far-reaching implications for measurement of quality, because CA investigates not only the skills achieved but also the conditions under which the skills were achieved, along with the community's participation in deciding which skills are relevant (Unterhalter 2007). The main challenge facing quality assessment in Kenya has long been the focus on a narrow set of outcomes, a residue of the World Bank's influence on educational policy. The Uwezo initiative has adopted a social justice approach focusing on redistribution, recognition and participation as its value basis with a broad-based perspective on outcomes that addresses the impact of socioeconomic and political structures on schooling, the effectiveness and efficiency of inputs into schooling, and the impact of teaching and learning processes on children's education. It also investigates marginalized groups in schooling, particularly rural-urban divides, gender, and remote communities when studying how inequality in the education system influences distribution of educational resources and outcomes. Moreover, it is based upon the participation of all stakeholders in the process of conceptualization and measurement. Education is thus conceived as a primary means of providing children with opportunities to pursue a good life and the capability to function in society, captured through the proxy indicators of numeracy and literacy, is the basis of measurement. Though still embedded in the human capital approach, NASMLA has also embraced the CA's focus on broad outcomes and the impact of contextual factors on these outcomes. However, NASMLA is still concerned with measuring enrolments and survival rates and also satisfying donor conditions rather than ensuring that children's outcomes from education are of relevance to their lives and well-being.

Inclusion entails the identification and acknowledgement of injustices against social groups and the CA explicitly recognizes the impact of conversion factors that hinder children's access to a quality education by perpetuating inequalities based on gender, class, race, ethnicity, language, disability, and urban-rural divides. Even though UPE is within reach in Kenya, many groups are in danger of being left behind due to the impact of these inequalities on their participation in schooling (UNESCO 2012). Uwezo has been quite effective in developing a framework that draws attention to the needs and requirements of learners from different socio-economic and cultural groups. The scheme has pursued inclusion of all children of school-going age in its assessment, even those who have never enrolled or who have dropped out of school, a population that has previously been ignored in many assessments, even though Kenya has more than a million children out of school (Uwezo 2012). In this, it outshines NASMLA which is still focused primarily on children in school. However, both focus on cultural and institutional barriers that restrict children's abilities to convert educational resources into valuable capabilities. Uwezo has been particularly successful in assessing the impact of language of instruction on learning, as in the case of rural children who are unable to communicate effectively in English due to lack of access to English language resources even though this is the language of instruction from Standard 1 onward. Uwezo has been at the vanguard in assessing real-life applications of the skills learnt in class in the children's daily lives. This is embodied in its aim to assess the meaningfulness of education to learners, families and the community and has been achieved by conducting assessment at home rather than in school, partly to capture all the children of school-going age, but also to provide the assessment with a real-life context when assessing the skills and capabilities of children. NASMLA is to a large extent still focused on the skill set encompassed by the KCPE exam and thus has yet to make any real connections between children's lives and the skills learnt in class.

In Kenyan education policy, there is rarely any participation by citizens and communities in decision-making on the form and content of education. This is because there is no facilitation of participation, particularly given the overwhelming influence of global development agendas. The CA places great emphasis on participatory democracy in social policy through democratic debate on decisions about which capabilities are relevant. Uwezo has again been at the forefront, holding wide consultative forums with different stakeholders such as children, parents, academics, government and civil society to develop a conceptualization of education quality that reflects the needs and realities of Kenyan communities. Furthermore, results from Uwezo's assessments are disseminated in the mass media and public forums at national, regional, county and village level to spark national debate on education quality. This participatory approach has also strengthened accountability and exposed various forms of corruption and abuse of power within the education system. NASMLA is, in contrast, a top-down development initiated mainly by the government as a response to the broad outcry over the deteriorating standards of education quality. Given its state-led approach, NASMLA falls short of providing for participation as it ignores the importance of including communities in the debate on what constitutes education quality.

Participation by stakeholders, including children, is important in developing a minimum threshold of quality that schooling should achieve, namely the capabilities to be pursued within basic education. Uwezo developed a minimum threshold of what a sufficiently good education should encompass through a participatory process that compiled views of different stakeholders as to which outcomes are to be valued, which resources should be harnessed to achieve this and which regional variations should be considered. This is essential in ensuring that human diversity is embedded in any final list of capabilities that is to be developed. The distinction between capabilities and functioning is a key to setting a minimum threshold for measurement of quality. While acknowledging that education should impart certain skills to children, it is necessary to avoid oversimplification into skills as favored in development orthodoxy. Whereas literacy and numeracy are important, it is essential to inquire whether the skills are relevant in enabling children to avoid capability deprivation, rather than mere resource deprivation. Dreze and Sen (2002: 7) define the capability of functioning as the basic minimum standard to be achieved by many social institutions such as schooling. Whereas the human capital approach measures the quality of education in terms of the generation of aggregate resources and personal resources that are valuable in enabling individuals to become productive on the labor market, the CA sets a threshold in enabling children to achieve the capability for functioning in society. Thus, even though literacy and numeracy are vital skills, the target of education should not be these skills per se, but rather the resources and freedoms children possess with which to convert these skills into essential functionings. Quality of education will then be evaluated accordingly in terms of the capabilities and functionings that are achieved because of it, rather than the resources or skills children are able to accumulate because of it. Uwezo not only pursues literacy and numeracy as essential outcomes of schooling, but also inquires as to whether the outcomes are of relevance to children in their daily lives. Examples of tasks assessed include employing numeracy skills to conduct transactions in a market and literacy skills to read informational posters on health and hygiene. NASMLA focuses on literacy and numeracy, but testing is restricted to academic environments and therefore fails to investigate whether these skills can be converted into functionings that enhance children's well-being. This restrictive nature is based on its policy antecedents, because it is derived from the Dakar Framework that, while acknowledging the multidimensional nature of educational quality, still restricts itself to an explicit focus on outcomes that are readily standardized.

In conclusion, it is evident that social justice requires the dismantling of institutional norms, discourses and practices that engender inequalities in access, participation and outcomes in education. This is relevant to education, in which policy and practice are shaped by national, political and socio-cultural norms that influence children's participation and outcomes. The CA is thus best suited to conceptualize and measure of education quality given its emphasis on capabilities in and through education that enable individuals to pursue lives of value to themselves. The language of capabilities reshapes the value and relevance of education in society by fostering debate on socio-economic and political norms that influence education quality. This approach satisfies the informational base required to sufficiently answer questions about what education quality is and how governments can engage with their citizens and communities in its pursuit. Although the human capital approach has long been the dominant ideology in the conceptualization and measurement of quality in Kenyan education, it lacks the requisite scope to take into account the Kenyan socio-economic and cultural context and provide an appropriate framework for education quality. Consistently low levels of quality in formal schooling and lack of relevance of the education to the livelihoods of learners attest to this insufficiency. CA on the other hand offers a conceptualization of education quality focused on achievement of educational and social justice not only through greater access and transitions but also through relevant curricula and pedagogy. Various initiatives aimed at conceptualizing, assessing and improving quality in the Kenyan education system are incorporating the tenets of CA into their design, even though this is sometimes not acknowledged explicitly. However, it is important to note that true success will be achieved only when implementation is followed through effectively in order to to avoid the implementation gap in which well-crafted policies are not adopted effectively in educational practice, a situation that is all too familiar in educational reforms in Kenya.

References

Appiah, Elizabeth/McMahon, Walter (2002): The social outcomes of education and feedbacks on growth in Africa. In: Journal of Development Studies, 38, 4, pp. 27–68.

Barrett, Angeline M./Chawla-Duggan, Rita/Lowe, John/Nikel, Jutta/Ukpo, Eugenia (2006): The concept of quality in education: A review of the international literature on the concept of quality in education. Bristol: EdQual.
Becker, Gary S. (1964): Human capital: A theoretical and empirical analysis, with special reference to education. Chicago: University of Chicago Press.
Drèze Jean/Sen, Amartya (2002): India: Development and participation. Oxford: OUP.
Gasper, Des/Van Staveren, Irene (2003): Development as freedom: And what else? In: Feminist Economics, 9, 2, pp. 137–161.
Hanushek, Eric A./Wößmann, Ludger (2008): Education quality and economic growth. Washington DC: World Bank.
Keeley, Brian (2007): OECD insights: Human capital. Paris: OECD.
Ministry of Education (2008): The development of education: The way of the future. Nairobi: Government Printer.
Ministry of Education (2011): In pursuit of quality: Policy dialogues and discourse on education quality in Kenya. Nairobi: Government Printer.
Ngware, Moses/Oketch, Moses/Ezeh, Alex (2010): Quality of primary education inputs in urban schools: Evidence from Nairobi. In: Education in Urban Society, 20, pp. 1–26.
Nussbaum, Martha (2000): Women and human development: The Capabilities Approach. Cambridge: Cambridge University Press.
Oduru, George/Bosu, Rosemary (2010). Leadership and management for change for quality improvement. Bristol: EdQual.
Ojiambo, Peter (2009): Quality of education and its role in national development: A case study of Kenya's educational reforms. In: Kenya Studies Review, 1, 1, pp. 133–149.
Psacharopoulos, George (1995): Building human capital for better lives. Washington DC: World Bank.
Robeyns, Ingrid (2005): Selecting capabilities for quality of life measurement. In: Social Indicators Research, 74, 1, pp. 191–215.
Roemer, Paul M. (1990): Human capital and growth: Theory and evidence. New York: Carnegie.
Sen, Amartya (1999): Development as freedom. Oxford: Oxford University Press.
Sifuna, Daniel (1990): Development of education in Africa: The Kenyan experience. Nairobi: Initiatives Publishers.
Tao, Sharon (2010): Applying the capability approach to school improvement interventions in Tanzania. London: EdQual.
Terzi, Lorella (2007): The capability to be educated. In: Walker, Melanie/Unterhalter, Elaine (eds.): Amartya Sen's Capability Approach and social justice in education. New York: Palgrave Macmillan, pp. 25–44.
Tikly, Leon (2010): Towards a framework for understanding the quality of education. Bristol: EdQual.
UNESCO (2006): EFA Global Monitoring Report: Literacy for life. Paris: UNESCO.
UNESCO (2012): EFA Global Monitoring Report: Youth and skills. Paris: UNESCO.
Unterhalter, Elaine (2003): Education, capabilities and social justice. Paris: UNESCO.
Unterhalter, Elaine (2007): Gender equality, education and the Capability Approach. In: Walker, Melanie/Unterhalter, Elaine (eds.): Amartya Sen's Capability Ap-

proach and social justice in education. New York: Palgrave Macmillan, pp. 87–108.

Uwezo (2012): Are our children learning: Annual learning assessment report. Nairobi: Uwezo.

Vaughan, Rosie (2007): Measuring capabilities. In: Walker, Melanie/Unterhalter, Elaine (eds.): Amartya Sen's Capability Approach and social justice in education. New York: Palgrave Macmillan, pp. 109–130.

Vos, Rob (1996): Educational indicators: What's to be measured? Washington DC: INDES.

Antoanneta Potsi

Greek Pre-primary Teachers' Beliefs and Practices: Are They Capabilities- or Performance-based?

1 Introduction

Teachers, being the front-line implementers of educational policy measures (Fullan 1989), play a crucial role in pedagogical praxis and the implementation of the curriculum. A plethora of scholars consider teachers' beliefs to be a major determinant of educational outcomes because these are associated with their respective practices (Fang 1996; Gess-Newsome 2002; Jones et al. 2000; Kagan 1992; Li/Rao 2009; McCarty et al. 2001; Mitchell/Hegde 2007; Pajares 1992; Vartuli 1999; Wang et al. 2008). However, policymakers reveal an implicit neglect and disregard of teachers' positioning into the educational frame that plays down their influential role in the formation of children's learning experiences. Despite living in the maelstrom of rhetoric over ameliorating the early childhood education and care system, preschool teachers are the last to be consulted and are marginalized from the planning and designing of curricula.

Within the Greek context, a number of scholars (Chrysafidis 2006; Doliopoulou 2000, 2002; Flouris/Pasias 2003; Frangos 2002; Koutsouvanou 2006; Sofou/Tsafos 2010; Sofou 2010) have stressed their concerns over the academic-goals-driven curriculum and their apprehensions about the schoolification of pre-primary school and its conversion into *"a misprint of primary school"* (Chrysafidis 2006).

In Greece, especially the introduction of the Cross-Thematic Curriculum Framework (CTCF) in 2001 – which outlines the direction for planning and developing activities in the context of the subjects of languages, mathematics, environmental studies, creation and expression, and computer science – was accompanied by intense criticism of the demand for the systematic application of specialized content in the aforementioned subjects in order to structure pre-school curriculum activities and the accompanying attempt to schoolify pre-primary school (Bikos 2005; Chrysafidis 2004, 2006; Doliopoulou 2002; Frangos 2002, 2005; Kiprianos 2007; Kitsaras 2004; Koutsouvanou 2006; Sofou 2010; Sofou/Tsafos 2010). Chrysafidis (2006) argues that by pursuing scientific knowledge, pre-primary school may be sacrificing creative activities and adopting similar tactics to those followed by primary teachers. Furthermore, Sofou and Tsafos (2010) report empirical evidence from a qualitative study indicating that teachers themselves are sceptical about those school-like learning areas of the curriculum that could lead to schoolification. However, it is not possible to estimate which aspects of this curriculum are being put into practice, because of the lack of empirical evidence on implementation and effectiveness, along with the lack of an evaluative framework of pedagogical practice from the Ministry of Education. The scarce research evidence in the field (Doliopoulou 1996; Sofou/Tsafos 2010) was the reason for this empirical study.

My study investigated pre-primary teachers' beliefs and practices regarding the actual curriculum approach being espoused in order to reveal what Shulman called the "missing programme" (cited in Gess-Newsome 2002: 3) in educational research. I used the broad early childhood curricular approaches that have been identified within the literature as a theoretical background. These twofold models or approaches in early childhood curricula mainly distinguish between a social pedagogic and a pre-primary stream. In addition, I sketch the linkages between the Capabilities Approach (CA) and early childhood education before outlining the analysis of teachers' beliefs and practices.

2 The two curricular approaches of Early Childhood Education

Moore (2008) presents the dimension on which approaches to early childhood services can be placed as being identified through the OECD thematic review of early childhood education and care policy (Bennett 2005; OECD 2006). This describes two broad curricular approaches: the social pedagogic approach and the pre-primary approach. As summarized by Bertrand (2007), social pedagogic practices, common in Scandinavian countries, New Zealand, and Italy, combine a broad developmental framework with local curriculum development. The focus is on developmental goals, interactivity with educators and peers, and a high quality of life in the early childhood setting. The curriculum sets broad orientations for the children while viewing the acquisition of developmental skills as a secondary and unplanned result of the curriculum. This approach is in contrast to the pre-primary practices common in France, the United Kingdom, and the United States that are characterized by centralized development of the curriculum – often with detailed goals and outcomes that determine or influence curriculum decisions about what and how children learn. The goals and outcomes are often stated as learning standards or learning expectations and are related to school readiness tasks and skills. Educators tend to interact with children around activities related to the identified learning expectations and rely more on direct instruction strategies. This approach, known as the pre-primary approach because the content of the curriculum mirrors what might be seen in primary school, is often referred to as the "schoolification"[1] of the early years (OECD 2006).

This debate has its origins in Bernstein's (1996) models of the curriculum, namely, performance and competence models. According to Bernstein, all curricula fall into one or the other category, and performance models of the curriculum are the most dominant around the world. The performance model has its origin in the behavioural objectives movement and clearly emphasizes marked subject boundaries, traditional forms of knowledge, explicit realization and recognition rules for pedagogic practice, as well as the designation and establishment of strong boundaries between different types of students. Implicit in this model is the sense that explicit criteria would save teachers and students from muddle and confusion. McLachlan et al. (2010) identify the Canadian (Ontario) curriculum and the UK Foundation Stage curriculum as indicative of this sort of curriculum model, because the former is quite explicit about the content it expects teachers to cover during the year before starting school and the latter has clearly defined curricular outcomes for very young children. In contrast to the performance model, the competence model suggests that learners have some control over the selection, pacing, and sequencing of the curriculum. According to McLachlan et al. (2010), New Zealand's early childhood curriculum, Te Whàriki (Ministry of Education 1996) is a good example of this sort of curriculum.

Recently, Liegle (2013) introduced a similar debate into the German context under a different terminology, that of *"Direkte und Indirekte Erziehung"*, whereas in the French context, Garnier (2009, 2012) refers to the phenomenon of *"scolarisation"* of the école maternelle which *may thus be analysed as a transformation of its objectives and curriculum to favour cognitive and language learning*. However, Nicolopoulou (2010) suggests that framing the

---

1 Nowadays, it seems that the emphasis given to the outcome achievement of education is gradually corroding early childhood education. The "academic" nature of the curriculum in many pre-primary classrooms stands out as one of the predominant issues in early childhood education as a consequence of the "new global discursive formation" of children and childhood that is being adapted in preschool legislation worldwide (Dahlberg 2009; Dahlberg/Moss 2005; Kascak/Pupala 2013; Penn 2002). The emphasis in pre-primary education has moved away from children's development and socialization towards the teaching of specific academic skills. Broström (2009) argues that the international political focus on learning in early childhood care and education – first of all on language and social competencies – aims to bring preschool closer to school, using as tools transition activities, strategies such as coherence in curricula, plus a closer collaboration between preschool teachers and school teachers in order to realize the idea of early learning. The challenge is illustrated succinctly by Moss and Bennett (2006: 2): "Globally, there is a tendency to treat early childhood services as junior partners, preparing children for the demands of formal schooling; this threatens what the Swedes call 'schoolification', the school imposing its demands and practices on other services, making them school-like."

alternatives as a dichotomy in which didactic/academic teaching is regarded as an opposite pole to unstructured free play is deeply misguided. Prout (2005: 11) points to the apparently increasing inability of oppositional dichotomies to provide a framework for understanding contemporary childhood. According to Bertrand (2007), in practice, most jurisdictions use approaches that blend elements of both, but lean towards either a pre-primary approach or a social pedagogic approach.

Within this debate, two approaches can be classified in early childhood education curricula: the pre-primary approach, the performance model, and the *Direkte Erziehung* description along with the *scolarisation* or schoolification phenomenon are classified under the term performance-based approach. Although the aforementioned terms are not synonymous, they do share a substantial number of similar characteristics such as the incorporation of academic learning. In contrast, the term capabilities-based approach synopsizes the social pedagogic approach, the competence model, or *Indirekte Erziehung*. The selection of the term "capabilities" is not random, because, in my view, the aforementioned conceptualizations encompass the principle of promoting children's capabilities enhancement in a holistic way and not unilaterally. The term is derived from the CA pioneered by Amartya Sen and further developed by Martha Nussbaum and a number of scholars.

3 The Capabilities Approach in Early Childhood Education

Nussbaum's approach (2006) uses the idea of a threshold level of each capability within a defined list of basic capabilities, beneath which it is held that truly human functioning is not available to citizens. The political goal should be understood in terms of getting citizens above this capability threshold. She identifies ten combined capabilities that, according to her, are central for human flourishing and a life of dignity and need to be present for a fully human "good life". These are: *1. Life. 2. Bodily health. 3. Bodily integrity. 4. Senses, imagination, thought. 5. Emotions. 6. Practical reason. 7. Affiliation. 8. Other species. 9. Play. 10. Control over one's environment.*

Although efforts have been made to operationalize the CA within the field of education (e.g. Terzi 2007; Walker/Unterhalter 2007), to date, the context of early childhood education has not been a matter of thorough debate. Nussbaum's philosophical conception of the CA may be of great relevance for the analysis of early childhood education and care, because some, if not all, of the identified core basic capabilities are met in a great number of early childhood curricula in which they are referred to either explicitly or implicitly.

Early childhood curricula sketch the concept of a good start in life based on the positioning of the agreed norms and values of a specific cultural setting. Furthermore, from this political work, one can derive the perspective or "resemblance" aims set for the next generation of this specific culture. If we consider Martha Nussbaum's list of central human capabilities as the minimum entitlements a person should have and compare this with the principles that govern early childhood education, one could easily realize that this normative evaluative framework is highly applicable in early childhood education. Many of the basic human capabilities have been scrutinized by scholars such as Montessori, Piaget, Vygotsky, Freud, or Fröbel, and these have produced an eminent argumentation on their indisputable value that continues to influence and shape early childhood education until today. Furthermore, a great number of early childhood curricula explicitly or implicitly endorse most of the central human capabilities. Some of these are considered in the Greek Cross-Thematic Curriculum Framework (CTCF) as well as in other curricula (e.g. Te Wariki, High Scope, Experimental Education, Lfpö 98 Swedish curriculum, Reggio Emilia approach, Norway's national curriculum, and the Finnish national curriculum guidelines on ECEC). With regard to the CTCF, the capabilities of play; senses, imagination, thought; emotions; and affiliation compose the essential means for the child's development and learning (Potsi 2013).

The debate over these aspects of childhood started with the ancient Greeks through the works of Plato and Aristotle and goes on till our days, revealing their interrelation as well as their instrumentality in child's development. Major theorists such as Piaget, Vygotsky, and Freud have been concerned with the meaning and the role of these components of human existence for the development of the child. Piaget and Vygotsky highlighted the importance of play, imagination, thinking, and socialization (part of which is the notion of affiliation). There is a strong interaction between emotional, social, and cognitive development in early childhood, and this depends upon environment and opportunity. Children can develop social-emotional competence through both planned and unplanned interactions with adults and peers. The child's free movement in space; his or her mental, creative, emotional, and imaginary expression and participation outside school in the present, or in established social frameworks of work in the future – these all constitute an axis for every present or future scheme pertaining to any preschool education strategy (Frangos 1993). Saito (2003) argues that education involves both instrumental and intrinsic values. However, the dominant case in early childhood curricula today tends to be that these capabilities play an instrumental role in serving academic knowledge acquisition and therefore the performance model of curriculum.

Tsatsaroni et al. (2003) claim that a basic characteristic of pre-school organization in many western societies for many decades has been its play-like activity. This has required teachers to structure the experiences of young children by acting upon the contexts of learning rather than the content. However, current policy initiatives and developments in a number of countries in the 1990s, including Greece, demand that teachers make systematic use of specialized content from science, mathematics, and other subjects to structure pre-school curriculum activities.

Biggeri et al. (2004) acknowledge the influence of teachers as well as parents or guardians on child development and capabilities. For Sen (1989: 54), education may well play a central role in the enhancement and development of capabilities. He argues (1999: 5) that the capabilities that adults enjoy are deeply conditional on their experience as children. The quality of childhood is important for future life but also for what happens in childhood; and it is inevitable that teachers influence children's childhoods in many diverse ways. Walker and Unterhalter (2007) emphasize the issue that occurs as a necessity according to Nussbaum: that of promoting a relevant capability "by requiring the functioning that nourishes it" (Nussbaum 2000: 91). They quote Nussbaum (2000: 91) who gives the example of requiring children to spend time in play, storytelling, and art activities as a way to promote the general capability of "play" that is important for adults. Their claim is that in children's and young people's education, it makes sense to consider people's functionings (what we manage to achieve) and not just capabilities.

4 Capabilities- or performance-based?

The aim of this study is to extend knowledge on how teachers' beliefs and their practices relate to the two sorts of curricular approach being followed in early childhood education – namely capabilities- and performance-based. Antecedent personal and contextual factors (years of experience, administrative control, decision latitude, self-efficacy) were included in the model in order to gain a better understanding of the social structures that restrict teachers' freedom of agency. Within this framework, I investigated the relationship between teachers' beliefs and their respective practices, and the preference for a specific sort of belief that teachers may favour.

Teachers' beliefs and practices have been associated with being developmentally appropriate or inappropriate (Charlesworth et al. 1991, 1993; Doliopoulou 1996; Hedge/Cassidy 2009; McCarty et al. 2001; Wang et al. 2008). However, other studies have also found inconsistencies between beliefs and practices (Vartulli 1999). Moreover, a study by Stipek and Byler (1997) revealed significant associations between beliefs and practices in child-centred versus more didactic, basic-skills approaches. Following these research findings, it is assumed that teachers will have a coherent set of beliefs that map on to the theoretical frameworks seen in each approach:

Capabilities-based beliefs represent the social-pedagogic approach in which the focus is on developmental goals, interactivity between pedagogues and children, and a high quality of life in the early childhood setting within a broad developmental framework and a local curriculum development. This approach offers broad orientations for children rather than prescribed outcomes, and the acquisition of developmental skills is perceived as a by-product rather than as the driver of the curriculum. The aim is to enhance children's capabilities in the emotional, social, aesthetic, and cognitive sector. Capabilities-based beliefs represent the respective acts through a spectrum of regarding children's capabilities enhancement as an intrinsic value in itself.

Performance-based beliefs represent the pre-primary or schoolification approach in which the curriculum, as a product of a centralized development, often contains detailed goals and outcomes stated as learning expectations, and these are related to school readiness tasks and skills. According to this approach, pedagogues tend to interact with children around activities related to these learning expectations and rely more on direct instruction strategies. The current Greek pre-primary curriculum espouses the pre-primary approach. Performance-based beliefs represent the respective capabilities as an instrument for the fulfilment of academic success and the achievement of academic objectives.

I hypothesize that capabilities-based beliefs have a negative effect on performance-based practices. This hypothesis is based on the assumption that due to the strong differences between the two sorts of pedagogy, it will be highly unlikely that capabilities-based beliefs will go hand in hand with performance-based beliefs. If teachers' beliefs are in accordance with their practices, as suggested in the research literature (Fang 1996; Kagan 1992; Stipek et al. 2001), then there should be a disharmony in the relationship between contradictory sorts of beliefs and practices. In the same line, this study aims to investigate performance-based beliefs in relation to capabilities-based practices. It examines the hypothesis that performance-based beliefs will relate negatively to capabilities-based practices.

My study aims to uncover the prevailing sort of belief in teachers' perceptions. Are teachers trying to implement the academic orientation emphasized in the Greek pre-primary curriculum, or do they believe in a capabilities-mode upbringing of children in which knowledge acquisition is a side effect of the process? I hypothesize that teachers' perceptions will tend to cohere around one of these two pedagogical dimensions. Answering this question will indicate whether or not the fears regarding the schoolification of Greek pre-primary schools are justified. This should end speculations on this topic and introduce much-needed empirical evidence to this debate.

The analysis was based on the data from 341 pre-primary teachers in Greece (333 women and 8 men; participation rate 70.3%).The sample contained novice (123) and well-experienced (218) teachers (see Katz 1972). The data were collected in three training and three retraining teacher programmes in diverse regions of Greece from October 2010 until January 2011. The selection of regions depended on the operation of the training and retraining programmes, namely *PEK* (Perifereiaka Epimorfotika Kentra)[2] and *Didaskaleia*,[3] and access to these institutions. These institutions offer government-subsidized training courses for in-service teachers.

I developed a questionnaire consisting of the measureable concepts used to operationalize the research hypotheses. The instrument was divided into three major categories: (a) background sociocultural information about teachers, (b) beliefs and practices rating scales, and (c) a professionalization scale from which self-efficacy and decision-latitude scales were derived.

With respect to the beliefs and practices rating scales, a self-reported format was used with a 4-point rating scale. The Beliefs Scale asked teachers to indicate the relative degree of importance for each statement on a rating scale ranging from 1 (*not important at all*) to 4 (*extremely important*), and the Practices Scale asked teachers to indicate the frequency for each statement on a scale ranging from 1 (*almost never*) to 4 (*very often*). For the original draft

---

[2] In its effort to increase and disseminate knowledge of developments in the field of in-service education and to reform the education system, the Greek Ministry of Education established a network of in-service teacher education centres (PEK) in 1985. PEKs offer a 100-teaching-hour programme in three sequential phases. These phases are structured around three main dimensions: cognitive, practical, and reflective. The attendance of the programme is mandatory and varies according to a teacher's length of service. The first phase lasts 60 hours for newly appointed teachers and 30 hours for substitute teachers. The second and third phases are attended by newly appointed teachers who, when entering the PEK, have less than 8 months of teaching experience in schools and have completed the first phase of introductory training. The introductory training programme addresses newly appointed primary and secondary school teachers as well as those hired as substitutes. The programme addresses an adult population that varies in terms of gender, age, basic university education, educational training and, most importantly, in terms of teaching experience.

[3] The purpose of Didaskaleio is to retrain and qualify preschool educators. In this context, the Didaskaleio of pre-primary educators seeks to monitor developments in educational science and educational technology in order to promote research, the production and transmission of knowledge, and experiences contributing to the educational development of the country in order to provide the necessary additional general and specific knowledge and skills that will ensure free and fair academic and professional careers for teachers in pre-primary education. Under the law, a pre-primary school teacher in either the public or private sector who has completed no less than 5 and no more than 25 years of educational service has the right to participate in the selection process for postgraduate studies at Didaskaleio (this also includes the years as substitute teacher in public education). The selection of teachers attending Didaskaleio is made by the Ministry of Education via written examinations. Attendance at a Didaskaleio is compulsory and teachers are released from their teaching duties. Those who successfully finish the biennial cycle of retraining in Didaskaleio receive a diploma in retraining in educational science.

version of this part of the questionnaire, I generated a pool of 49 and 19 items containing statements on aspects of children's learning for beliefs and practices respectively. The item statements derived their content from the aforementioned capabilities, namely senses, imagination, and thought; emotions; affiliation; and play. In the case of the performance-based items, these capabilities were conceptualized as an instrument to teach the respective learning content (academic learning acquisition), whereas in the capabilities-based case, items stressed the value of the respective capabilities as an end in itself (capabilities enhancement). I anticipated that teachers who favoured a capabilities-based approach might respond quite differently to each of these statements in comparison with teachers who favoured a more performance-based approach.

The items chosen for the Teachers' Beliefs Scale were influenced by the professional literature and were adjusted to the requirements of the Greek Cross-Thematic Curriculum Framework (CTCF). Scale reliability testing using Cronbach's alpha coefficients (α) (Table 1) and measurement model validation using confirmatory factor analysis (CFA)[4] were conducted with AMOS 20. Results showed that all scales yielded fairly good reliability (α ranged from .60–.88). To construct the measurement models, scale items were used as indicators (manifest variables) for each measurement model. The results of CFA revealed that the measurement models yielded good fit indices (e.g. $\chi^2/df < 2.00$; $p > .03$; GFI[5] & CFI[6] $> .90$; RMR[7] $< .05$) and revealed positively significant factor loadings (β).

The conceptual model of the current study was sketched on the basis of a literature review describing a system of links among the variables. A cutting-edge technique in multivariate analysis – structural equation modelling (SEM) – was employed to investigate the first- and second-order factor models of this study empirically by conducting confirmatory factor analyses (see Potsi 2013 for details on the study).

---

[4] Confirmatory factor analysis (CFA) is a theory- or hypothesis driven analysis that allows researchers to test hypotheses about a particular factor structure. CFA is the basis of the measurement model in full structural equation modeling (SEM) and can be estimated using SEM software (see Albright/Myoung Park 2009).
[5] Goodness of Fit Index (GFI)
[6] According to Albright and Myoung Park (2009: 6f.), the "comparative fit index (CFI) evaluates 'the fit of a user-specified solution in relation to a more restricted, nested baseline model', in which the 'covariances among all input indicators are fixed to zero' or no relationship among variables is posited. CFI ranges from 0 for a poor fit to 1 for a good fit."
[7] Root Mean Square Residual (RMR)

Table 1: Scales reliabilities

Scales	Sample item	A (N_{item})	B	Measurement model fit indices				
				χ^2/df	P	GFI	CFI	RMR
1. Teachers' Beliefs Scale								
1.1. Capabilities-based beliefs (BCA)	It is not at all/not that/significantly/extremely/ important for the children to come up with possible alternative solutions during problem-solving activities.	.83 (24)	.42 - .79	1.48	.18	.99	.99	.00
1.2. Performance-based beliefs (BAG)	It is not at all/not that/significantly/extremely/ important for the children to improve their mathematical skills.	.75 (19)	.39 - .69	.84	.58	.99	1.00	.01
	Total	.84 (43)						
2. Teachers' practices scale								
2.1. Capabilities-based practices	How often do children play freely?	.63 (7)	.39 - .69	1.93	.03	.98	.95	.01
2.2. Performance-based practices	How often do you involve/engage children in activities focusing on the acquisition of mathematical skills?	.60 (6)	.30 - .61	1.88	.06	.99	.95	.01
	Total	.67 (13)						

Source: own data collection

5 Discussion of the empirical findings

The data analysis indicated that teachers' beliefs were in accordance with their self-reported actions. More specifically, teachers' capabilities-based beliefs predicted capabilities-based practices, whereas teachers' performance-based beliefs predicted performance-based practices. This is consistent with the widely expressed argument that teachers' beliefs influence their teaching practices (Fang 1996; Kagan 1992; Stipek et al. 2001). Furthermore, the predictor constructs, namely, years of experience, administrative control, self-efficacy, and decision latitude, significantly influenced teachers' beliefs. However, whereas the antecedent factors of years of experience, administrative control, and decision latitude significantly predicted teachers' performance-based beliefs, this was not the case for capabilities-based beliefs. Teachers' self-efficacy had significantly positive direct effects on both sorts of belief – namely, capabilities- and performance-based – indicating that teachers' belief in their ability to have a positive effect on children's development and learning is a significant factor for both pedagogical stances (see Potsi 2013).

The second-order model of teachers' beliefs showed that the prevailing sort of belief in Greek teachers' perceptions was the capabilities-based one (Figure 1). It seems that teachers tend to favour a more pedagogical approach in which the enhancement of children's capabilities is prioritized rather than the over-emphasis on mere academic skills acquisition. This delivers a solid statement that could lead to an optimistic view on the fears of schoolification of the Greek pre-primary school raised by scholars.

Despite the curriculum demand from teachers to make systematic use of specialized content from science, mathematics, and other subjects to structure pre-primary activities, they are still capabilities-driven, prioritizing a social pedagogic approach and emphasizing children's capabilities expansion. This result does not imply by any means that performance-based sort of beliefs are disregarded and/or overlooked. Performance-based beliefs were also appreciated but on a minor level. The association between the two sorts of beliefs could be characterized as an interrelation because it seems that teachers value a combinatory approach between the two stances (Potsi 2013).

Figure 1: Second-order model of teachers' overarching beliefs

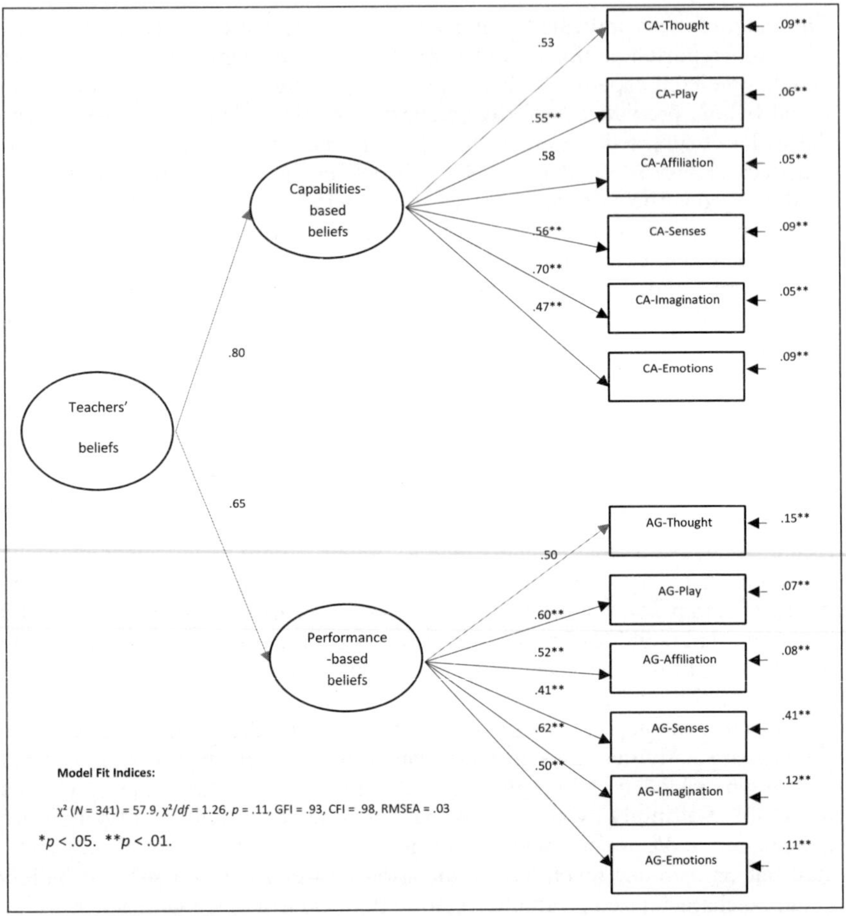

[Figure: Second-order CFA model. "Teachers' beliefs" loads on "Capabilities-based beliefs" (.80) and "Performance-based beliefs" (.65).

Capabilities-based beliefs loadings on indicators:
- CA-Thought: .53, error .09**
- CA-Play: .55**, error .06**
- CA-Affiliation: .58, error .05**
- CA-Senses: .56**, error .09**
- CA-Imagination: .70**, error .05**
- CA-Emotions: .47**, error .09**

Performance-based beliefs loadings on indicators:
- AG-Thought: .50, error .15**
- AG-Play: .60**, error .07**
- AG-Affiliation: .52**, error .08**
- AG-Senses: .41**, error .41**
- AG-Imagination: .62**, error .12**
- AG-Emotions: .50**, error .11**

Model Fit Indices:

χ^2 (N = 341) = 57.9, χ^2/df = 1.26, p = .11, GFI = .93, CFI = .98, RMSEA = .03

*p < .05. **p < .01.]

Source: own illustration

The CFA analysis revealed that pre-primary teachers' perceptions of these two constructs did not cluster in a dichotomy. Their association could be better characterized as an interrelation or better, as Liegle (2013) argues a *dialogic* relation, because it seems that teachers value an approach combining both stances. This is in line with Bertand's (2007) argument that, in practice, most education systems use approaches that blend elements of both, but lean towards either a pre-primary or a social pedagogic approach. Based on her argument, it can be inferred from the data of my study that Greek pre-primary teachers lean towards a social pedagogic approach, because findings show that the capabilities-based beliefs prevail in teachers' thinking. This result was expected, because it was assumed that both these two constructs, representing as they do two widely discussed trends in the field of early childhood education, would influence teachers' thinking and perceptions. This finding leads to the conclusion that capabilities- and performance-based beliefs are both appreciated by the teachers. This should be taken into account in further research. In sum, teachers are likely to choose a middle or interactive position in which they are able to recognize and perceive practices that are appropriate for the instructional circumstances and for the needs of the children in their care.

6   Conclusions

Teachers' beliefs are important to understand classroom practices. Teachers, as professionals and front-line implementers, should be included in the development of a pre-primary school that offers an adequate environment in which children may flourish. The challenge of improving one's ways of working to better serve the interests of children and the community is also accomplished by studying teachers' beliefs and how they bring that knowledge to life in their classrooms. This study has served to initiate the process of gathering information on Greek pre-primary teachers' beliefs and practices, and it has opened the path to unveiling the actual curriculum in Greek pre-primary school. Its importance is both theoretical and practical, because it contributes to our understanding of teachers' thinking, particularly since the importance of pre-primary experiences is well acknowledged. Certainly, teachers' beliefs and practices impact on the quality of children's pre-primary experience and on the current benefits that it brings to children. My study provided data in an area in which there has been much speculation but little empirical evidence.

To sum up, this study has delivered insights into the conglomerate of teachers' beliefs and practices. For the Greek context, pre-primary teachers favour more capabilities-based beliefs although without disregarding performance-based beliefs. This leads to the conclusion that the fear expressed over the schoolification of Greek pre-primary school does not seem, up to now, to be justified empirically. Finally, three factors were identified as predictors of performance-based beliefs, namely, teachers' years of experience, administrative control, and decision latitude. In conclusion, this study provided data in an area in which there has been much speculation but scarce empirical evidence. It has opened the path to unveiling the actual curriculum implemented and responds to the fears regarding the schoolification of pre-primary school. The data should be taken into consideration in future educational reform, policy implementation, and the design of training. The take-home message of this research is that by imposing an educational reform in a top-down direction without taking into account the front-line implementers' views, its successful implementation is still questionable despite the enormous resources invested in teacher training.

References

Albright, Jeremy J./Myoung Park, Hun (2009): Confirmatory factor analysis using Amos, LISREL, Mplus, SAS/STAT CALIS. Working Paper. The University Information Technology Services (UITS) Center for Statistical and Mathematical Computing, Indiana University. Retrieved from: http://www.indiana.edu/~statmath/stat/all/cfa/index.html

Bennett, John (2005): Curriculum issues in national policy-making. In: European Early Childhood Education Research Journal, 13, 2, pp. 5–23.

Bernstein, Basil (1996): Class and pedagogies: visible and invisible. In: Educational Studies, 1, 1, pp. 23–41.

Bertrand, Jane (2007): Preschool programs: Effective curriculum. Comments on Kagan and Kauerz and on Schweinhart. In: Tremblay, Richard E./Barr, Ronald G./Peters, Ray DeV. (eds.): Encyclopedia on Early Childhood Development [online]. Montreal, Quebec: Centre of Excellence for Early Childhood Development; 2007: 1–7. Available at: http://www.child-encyclopedia.com/documents/BertrandANGxp.pdf. Accessed [01/09/2011].

Biggeri, Mario/Libanora, Renato/Mariani, Stefano/Menchini, Leonardo (2004): Children establishing their capabilities: preliminary results of the survey during the first children's world congress on child labour. Paper presented at the 4th International Conference on the Capability Approach, "Enhancing Human Security", University of Pavia, Italy (unpubl.).

Bikos, Konstantinos (2005): Aspects of the curriculum in the context of the cross-thematic approach. In: Germanos, Dimitrios/Panajiotidou, Eleftheria/Bikos, Konstantinos/Birbili, Maria (eds.): Proceedings of the Panhellenic Conference "The cross-thematic approach of teaching and learning in preschool and primary school age, OMEP & TEPAE AUT (pp. 52–59). Athens: Ellinika Grammata (in Greek).

Broström, Stig (2009): Early childhood education – actual positions and future possibilities. Paper presented at the conference "Konturen frühpädagogischer Hochschulbildung – Forschung, Lehre und Praxis verzahnen". Berlin, Germany: Robert Bosch Foundation (unpubl.).

Charlesworth, Rosalind/Hart, Craig H./Burts, Diane C./Hernandez, Sue (1991): Kindergarten teachers' beliefs and practices. In: Early Child Development and Care, 70, 1, pp. 17–35.

Charlesworth, Rosalind/Hart, Craig H./Burts, Diane C./Thomasson, Renee H./Mosley, Jean/Fleege, Pamela O. (1993): Measuring the developmentally appropriateness of kindergarten teachers' beliefs and practices. In: Early Childhood Research Quarterly, 8, 3, pp. 255–276.

Christenson, Sandra L./Rounds, Theresa/Gorney, Deborah (1992): Family factors and student achievement: An avenue to increase students' success. In: School Psychology Quarterly, 7, 3, pp. 178–206.

Chrysaphidis, Konstantinos (2004): Epistemological principles of preschool education: The preschool in the space of ideology and science. Athens: typothito – Giorgos Dardanos.

Chrysaphidis, Konstantinos (2006): The new curriculum of the Greek kindergarten: Innovations in service of DEPPS. In: Modern Kindergarten, 53, 1, pp. 108–115.

Dahlberg, Gunilla (2009): Policies in early childhood education and care: potentialities for agency, play and learning. In: Qvortrup, Jens/Corsaro, William A./Honig, Michael-Sebastian (eds.): The Palgrave Handbook of Childhood Studies. Basingstoke: Palgrave Macmillan, pp. 228–237.

Dahlberg, Gunilla/Moss, Peter (2005): Ethics and politics in early childhood education. Contesting early childhood. New York, NY: Routledge Falmer.

Doliopoulou, Elsie (2000): The new curriculum for the kindergarten: some first thoughts. In: Modern Kindergarten, 26, 1, pp. 72–77.

Doliopoulou, Elsie (2002): The full-day kindergarten and the Unified Cross-Thematic Curriculum Framework on kindergarten (DEPPS). In: Modern kindergarten, 35, 1, pp. 8–12.

Doliopoulou, Elsie (2006): System of early education/care and professionalization in Greece, SEEPRO Report, 1–19. Retrieved from http://www.ifp.bayern.de/imperia/md/content/stmas/ifp/commissioned_report_greece.pdf.

Fang, Zhihui (1996): A review of research on teacher beliefs and practices. In: Educational Research, 38, 1, pp. 47–65.

Flouris, George/Pasias, George (2003): A critical appraisal of curriculum reform in Greece (1980–2002): Trends, challenges, and perspectives. In: European Education, 35, 3, pp. 73–90.

Frangos, Christos (1993): A Child Development Centre (C.D.C.) based on the world of work and everyday life: A case of quality education provision for 2.5–5 year old children. In: European Early Childhood Education Research Journal, 1, 1, pp. 41–52.

Frangos, Christos (2002): Διάλογος για την παιδεία και την εκπαίδευση: τα φροντιστήρια με τα ευρώ και προγράμματα σπουδών για φροντιστήρια. Σύγχρονη Εκπαίδευση, 122, 1, pp. 22–32.

Frangos, Christos (2005): The curricula and the «new» study programs. In: Modern Education, 125, 1, pp. 60–68. (in Greek: Διάλογος για την παιδεία και την εκπαίδευση: Τα αναλυτικά προγράμματα και τα «νέα» προγράμματα σπουδών, Σύγχρονη Εκπαίδευση)

Fullan, M. (1989): Implementing educational change: What we know. PHREE Background Paper Series, Document No. PHREE/89/18. Retrieved from http://www-wds.worldbank.org/external/default/WDSContentServer/WDSP/IB/1989/07/01/000009265_3960929042553/Rendered/PDF/multi_page.pdf.

Garnier, Pascale (2009): Préscolarisation ou scolarisation? L'évolution institutionnelle et curriculaire de l'école maternelle. In: Revue française de pédagogie, 169, 1, pp. 5–15.

Garnier, Pascale (2012): Preschool education in France: scolarisation of the ecole maternelle and schoolification of family life. In: Pedagogy – theory & praxis, 5, 1, pp. 43–53.

Gess-Newsome, Julie (2002): Pedagogical content knowledge: An introduction and orientation. In: Contemporary Trends and Issues in Science Education, 6, 1, pp. 3–17.

Hedge, Archana/Cassidy, Deborah J. (2009): Teachers' beliefs and practices regarding developmentally appropriate practices: a study conducted in India. In: Early Childhood Development and Care, 179, 7, pp. 837–847.

Jones, Lynda D./Burts, Diane C./Buchanan, Teresa K./Jambunathan, Saigeetha (2000): Beginning prekindergarten and kindergarten teachers' beliefs and practices: supports and barriers to developmentally appropriate practices. In: Journal of Early Childhood Teacher Education, 21, 3, pp. 397–410.

Kagan, Dona M. (1992): Implications of research on teacher belief. In: Educational Psychologist, 27, 1, pp. 65–90.

Kascak, Ondrej/Pupala, Branislav (2013): Buttoning up the gold collar – the child in neoliberal visions of early education and care. In: Human Affairs, 23, 1, pp. 319–337.

Katz, Lilian G. (1972). Developmental stages of preschool teachers. Clearinghouse on Early Childhood Education, Urbana, Illinois. Retrieved from http://eric.ed.gov/PDFS/ED057922.pdf

Kiprianos, Pandelis (2007): Child, family, society: the history of preschool education from its beginnings to our present days. Gutenberg – Giorgos & Kostas Dardanos: Athens (in Greek).

Kitsaras, Georgios (2004): Programs and methodology of preschool didactics. Self-published.

Koutsouvanou, E. (2006): Some views on the Unified Cross-Thematic Curriculum Framework (DEPPS). In: Modern Kindergarten, 53, 1, pp. 96–106.

Li, Hui/Rao, Nirmala (2009): Multiple literacies: beliefs and related practices among Chinese kindergarten teachers. In: Knowledge Management & E-Learning: An International Journal, 1, 4, pp. 269–284.

Liegle, Ludwig (2013): Frühpädagogik: Erziehung und Bildung kleiner Kinder – Ein dialogischer Ansatz. Stuttgart: Kohlhammer.

McCarty, Frances/Abbott-Shim, Martha/Lambert, Richard (2001): The relationship between teacher beliefs and practices, and Head Start classroom quality. In: Early Education and Development, 12, 2, pp. 225–238.

McLachlan, Claire/Fleer, Marilyn/Edwards, Susan (2010): Early Childhood Curriculum. Planning, assessment and implementation. Melbourne. Cambridge University Press.

Ministry of Education (1996): Te Whàriki – He Whàriki Màtauranga mò ngà Mokopuna o Aotearoa – Early Childhood Curriculum. Learning Media Wellington. New Zealand.

Mitchell, Linda Crane/Hedge, Archana V. (2007): Beliefs and practices of in-service preschool teachers in inclusive settings: implications for personnel preparation. In: Journal of Early Childhood Teacher Education, 28, 4, pp. 353–366.

Moore, Tim G. (2008): Towards an early years learning framework for Australia. CCCH Working Paper 4 (August 2008). Parkville, Victoria: Centre for Community Child Health.
Moss, Peter/Bennett, John (2006): Toward a new pedagogical meeting place? Bringing early childhood into the education system. Briefing paper for a Nuffield Educational Seminar, 26 September 2006. Retrieved from http://89.28.209.149/fileLibrary/pdf/briefingpaper_Moss_Bennett.pdf.
Nicolopoulou, Ageliki (2010): The alarming disappearance of play from early childhood education. In: Human Development, 53, 1, pp. 1–4.
Nussbaum, Martha (2000): Women and human development: The capabilities approach. Cambridge: Cambridge University Press.
Nussbaum, Martha (2006): Education and democratic citizenship: Capabilities and quality education. In: Journal of Human Development, 7, 3, pp. 385–395.
OECD (2006): Starting Strong II: early childhood education and care. OECD Publishing: Paris.
Pajares, Frank (1992): Teachers' beliefs and educational research: Cleaning up a messy construct. In: Review of Educational Research, 62, 3, pp. 307–332.
Penn, Helen (2002): The World Bank's view of early childhood. In: Childhood, 9, 1, pp. 118–132.
Potsi, Antoanneta (2013): Pre-primary education from the perspective of the capability approach: an empirical investigation into teachers' beliefs and self-reported practices. Retrieved from: http://pub.uni-bielefeld.de/publication/2577603.
Prout, Alan (2005): The future of childhood: towards an interdisciplinary study of children. London: Routledge Falmer.
Saito, Madoka (2003): Amartya Sen's capability approach to education: A critical exploration. In: Journal of Philosophy of Education, 37, 1, pp. 17–33.
Sen, Amartya (1989): Development as capability expansion. Retrieved from: http://morgana.unimore.it/Picchio_Antonella/Sviluppo%20umano/svilupp%20umano/Sen%20development.pdf
Sen, Amartya (1999): Breaking the poverty cycle – investing in early childhood. Keynote Address, Inter-American Development Bank, Sustainable Development Department, Social Department Division. Paris, March 14, 1999. Retrieved from: http://www.unicef.org/lac/spbarbados/Implementation/ECD/BreakingPovertyCycle_ECD_1999.pdf
Sofou, Efstratia (2010): Recent trends in early childhood curriculum: The case of Greek and English national curricula. In: Mattheou, Dimitris (ed.): Changing educational landscapes: Educational policies, schooling systems and higher education – a comparative perspective. Dordrecht: Springer, pp. 227–240.
Sofou, Efstratia/Tsafos, Vassilios (2010): Preschool teachers' understandings of the national preschool curriculum in Greece. In: Early Childhood Education Journal, 37, 1, pp. 411–420.
Stipek, Deborah/Byler, Patricia (1997): Early childhood education teachers: Do they practice what they preach? In: Early Childhood Research Quarterly, 12, 1, pp. 305–325.
Stipek, Deborah/Givvin, Karen B./Salmon, Julie M./MacGyvers, Valanne L. (2001): Teachers' beliefs and practices related to mathematics instruction. In: Teaching and Teacher Education, 17, 2, pp. 213–226.

Terzi, Lorella (2007): The capability to be educated. In: Walker, Melanie/Unterhalter, Elaine (eds.): Amartya Sen's capability approach and social justice in education. New York, NY: Palgrave Macmillan, pp. 25–43.

Tsatsaroni, Anna/Ravanis, Konstantinos/Falaga, Anna (2003): Studying the recontextualisation of science in pre-school classrooms: Drawing on Bernstein's insights into teaching and learning practices. In: International Journal of Science and Mathematics Education, 1, pp. 385–417.

Vartuli, Sue (1999): How early childhood teacher beliefs vary across grade level. In: Early Childhood Research Quarterly, 14, 4, pp. 489–514.

Walker, Melanie/Unterhalter, Elaine (2007): The capability approach: Its potential for work in education. In: Walker, Melanie/Unterhalter, Elaine (eds.): Amartya Sen's Capability Approach and social justice in education. London: Palgrave Macmillan, pp. 1–18.

Wang, Jianhong/Elicker, James/McMullen, Mary/Mao, Shuyang (2008): Chinese and American preschool teachers' beliefs about early childhood curriculum. In: Early Child Development and Care, 178, 3, pp. 227–249.

Lakshmi N. Venkataraman[1]

Caste, Class, and Education: Intersectional Implications of Capability Formation in a South Indian Village

1 Introduction

India, as an ethnographic museum, is known for the national notion of *unity in diversity*. It is a country of many religions, further divided in terms of diverse social hierarchies. The socio-economic reality of India is not based on class dynamics alone. It intersects with factors such as caste that play an important role in these dynamics. Against this backdrop, the central argument in this chapter conceptualizes the primordial identities of caste and its interrelationships with the economic factors of class. This interrelationship is conceptualized in terms of intersectionality in the social sphere. The concept of intersection attempts to underscore how the diverse social positions interact in educational functionings in Sripuram. As intersectionality is "the mutually constitutive relations among social identities" (Shields 2008: 301), the interactions of caste, class, and education are conceptualized in understanding the capability formation.

The stratification of caste as a social system in India places individuals hierarchically according to their birth. Inheritance based on birth in the caste structure most often marks a "fixed" identity on individuals in whom social mobility is discouraged. The broader classification of *varnashrma dharma* divides people in terms of Brahmins, Kshatriyas, Vaishyas, and Shudras. This *ascriptive* social order based on the Hindu scriptures places Brahmins (or the erstwhile "higher" castes) above the "others". Kshatriyas, who are traditionally known for martial valour and managerial roles, are in the next layers of social stratification. Third, the Vaishyas, who are known for their trade and commerce activities, are above the last layer of the "lower" castes. In the fourfold ascriptive division of labour, the "lower" castes are often addressed as Shudras (or Dalits or Harijans).[2] The ascriptive nature of the caste system

---

[1] Lakshmi N. Venkataraman works at the Centre for Research on Higher Education and Development at the University of the Free State, South Africa.
[2] In Sripuram, the Pallars are the erstwhile lower castes who are addressed as Dalits in the village.

is, thus, unique in a stratification through which an individual's social status is determined mostly by birth.[3] It must be noted that the present-day Indian state considers caste as a marker for "protective" public policies in education and employment.

Against this backdrop, the central analysis of this chapter is based on ethnographic fieldwork conducted in a south Indian village pseudonymously named Sripuram in Tamil Nadu. Because the chapter has been influenced conceptually by the Capability Approach (CA) (Sen 1999), the basic aim is to highlight the complex interactions between human agencies and social structure. For this, qualitative data and *reflexive* insights have been collected from Sripuram. This village, it must be noted, was studied by a renowned Indian sociologist Andre Beteille in the 1960s. He conducted his social anthropological fieldwork on *caste, class*, and *power* dimensions (Beteille 1965). By revisiting the same village nearly five decades later, the chapter analyses the intersections of *caste, class, and education* in capability formation.

As a complex system, intersectionality assumes a methodology that "sees everything as interactions, not 'main effects'" (Choo/Ferree 2010: 136) the current chapter highlights the in/tangible structural factors in educational outcome in the village. An intersection-based analysis offers "insights missed in even excellent sociological work" (Choo/Ferree 2010: 130) and is crucial when even the acclaimed academic works of M. N. Srinivas and Beteille have overlooked these dimensions.[4] This limitation is not a conscious self-restriction on the scholars' part, because one must acknowledge the currently emerging interest in intersectional research studies. Methodologically, intersectionality-specific research has yet to capture mainstream research. Although the feminist discourse is discussing it in India, the present work extends it to analyse the factors of caste, class, and education. This is essential given the sociological reality that India is one of the most stratified societies in the world.[5] The structure of the chapter, with this background, is organized to give a contextualization of Sripuram before discussing the intersectionality in detail.

---

3   Each layer in the fourfold classification is a conglomeration of diverse caste groups that often has *endogamous* rules and regulations. Even today, these rules often determine other social aspects including commensality.

4   This has been acknowledged by Beteille himself in personal interviews with the author. In his view, gender is one important dimension that "slipped out" of the central focus in his work.

5   Although this is an inheritance-based *division of labour*, one can find a complicated picture of variations across the regions in the country. In the present context in Sripuram, the villagers have been broadly classified into three groups: the Brahmins (at the top), followed by the OBCs or the Other Backward Classes (a combination of variety of middle level castes), with the Pallar (who are often mentioned as Scheduled Castes or the SCs; Dalits and also sometimes be called as Harijans) at the bottom of the caste hierarchy.

2 Situating Sripuram

Sripuram is one of the small villages of Tamil Nadu in south India. It is located on the banks of river Kaveri. Although, Sripuram is an anonymized name for ethnographic reasons, the location of the village was introduced to the author by Professor Andre Beteille. Through his fieldwork in 1960s, it must be noted, Beteille produced one of the eminent sociological texts on India. His oft-cited book "Caste, Class and Power" is based on this multi-caste village (Beteille 1965).[6]

Like any other village in Tamil Nadu, Sripuram is inhabited by diverse socio-economic groups and characterized by the presence of different castes. Sripuram is a small village of nearly 380 households containing around 1,500 people. According to the present author's population survey, there are nearly 65 Brahmin houses, 209 non-Brahmin houses, and 103 Scheduled Castes houses in the village. The physical location of the village is divided in terms of diverse streets that are occupied mainly along caste lines. For instance, the *Agraharam*, where the erstwhile "higher" caste or the Brahmins live, "welcome" anyone who enters the village from outside. This is parallel to other streets on which the fellow villagers of other social groups live. For instance, the Other Backward Classes (henceforth OBCs), who are often addressed as "dominant castes" (Srinivas 1987), live in the nearby streets next to the Agraharam.[7] The OBCs are the conglomeration of diverse caste groups of Kallar, Padayachi, and Vellalars among others in the village. Socio-economically, they occupy the middle layer between the extreme social positions of the Brahmins and the Pallars. Pallars, who historically occupy the lower rung of the socio-economic hierarchy, are often addressed either as Scheduled Castes (SCs) or Dalits in the village. Their erstwhile social position on the lower rungs of the hierarchy seems to be the reason for their economic deprivation. For instance, they represent almost all indicators of *ill-being* in the village. These include economic deprivation, illiteracy, unemployment, and also educated under-employment.

The physical presence of these three broader classifications of social groups of Brahmins, non-Brahmins (or OBCs), and Pallars reveals their distinct lifestyles that differ remarkably from each other. Although the OBCs and Pallars are physically identical to the foreigners, one can observe nearly invisible forms of social unrest between them. These unrests are often dis-

---

6 The author wishes to thank Professor Beteille for his sustained support for the current research work in Sripuram.
7 The concept of dominant caste is sociologically important. Srinivas (1987) defined this in terms of three crucial variables: the numerical strength, politics, and economic position of a caste. In this work, it denotes the OBCs who constitute a conglomeration of diverse caste groups in terms of numerical strength and political influence in the village who also possess economic power due to their landholdings in Sripuram.

played to establish primordial identities; it is essential to mention the social distancing of Brahmins from all "others" in the village. Their self-withdrawal from the *everyday* interaction order cannot be challenged legally due to their exclusivist lifestyles. Furthermore, it has to be mentioned that the visible forms of discrimination have often been countered by both academics and activists in the country. The invisible forms such as exclusivist lifestyles have, however, been an adaptive "backlash" by the status quo social structure.

In light of this exclusivism, the Brahmins of Sripuram, like anywhere else in the country, are generally known for their education capital through which they have historically occupied the higher echelons of the power structure. This is visible in terms of their socio-economic status in the village. This has been possible because they owned most of the land in the village till a few decades back. The descriptions of Beteille have often addressed them as the *Mirasdars* or landowners in his work (Beteille 1965). This has given them power to "control" the "others" who are economically dependent on their landholdings. The intersection of socio-economic aspects in relation to education has ensured their growth and development over the years. For instance, Brahmin women are most often relatively well-educated and more knowledgeable than the men of other castes in the village. This is in contrast to the general presumption that women occupy the lower rungs of the patriarchal hierarchy. In a similar vein, Brahmin men are comparatively superior in their education and development indicators whereby the intersection of caste and class plays an essential role.

3   Intersectionality of caste and class

The primordial identities of caste and its sociological implications for the class positions of individuals have a conceptual importance for the intersectional analysis in the country. Beteille has presented analyses of caste and class factors in Sripuram. The class system in his view "overlaps to a considerable extent with the caste structure, but also cuts across it at a number of points" (Beteille 1965: 4). As convergence between these factors is structurally continuing even today, "there has been considerable modification of the traditional congruent relationships between caste and social class" (Mencher 1970: 210). The result is that the capability formation of the human agencies is conditioned by both the intersectional factors in the village as well as the wider socio-economic contexts of the country. The notion of capability must be defined against this backdrop. Capabilities depend on the competencies or life skills learned in education. This is primarily important for analysing the broader notions of *freedom* or the ability to take independent decisions. The importance of capabilities has consequently been understood in light of their effects on the cycle of economic deprivation and social exclusion. This vicious cycle seemingly reinforces the powers and privileges within the village.

The current forms of caste and class, as a consequence of the social changes, have to be contrasted with the earlier descriptions of Sripuram. For instance, in contrast to the description in which "a villager's caste determined his position in the class system and power hierarchy" (Nandy 1966: 729), this has increasingly been subsumed by the educational status of individuals today. Consequently, one can observe a growing dissociation of caste and class in the village. This dissociation, in the words of D'Souza, is due mainly to the emerging social changes:

With the change from a static, traditional social order to a more dynamic one, the economic and political systems gradually detach themselves from caste and acquire a more autonomous character. (D' Souza 1999: 301)

The class positions, in this newer form, are often determined by occupational outcomes in which the role of education is increasingly *instrumental* in India. In addition, Driver's findings point to the:

Considerable independence between social class and the caste hierarchy, between caste and several status-groupings, and between social class and some status-groupings. Such independence means that the concept of "status summation" has quite limited applicability today in urban South India. (Driver 1982: 251)

As this underlines the importance of the intersection, it is also pertinent to mention Delige's analysis:

The problem of class in rural India has historically been twofold: first, castes have corresponded only very imperfectly to social classes, and second, the analysis of Indian society in terms of classes has been particularly fraught because of the non-recognition of such categories by Indians themselves. However, class analysis may be increasingly useful today. (Deliege 2011: 52)

Against this backdrop, the first noticeable change in the village is now the working relationship between the OBCs and the Pallars. This runs counter to the caste-based economic interdependence of earlier times when the Pallars used to work for the landowners or the *Mirasdars* as agricultural labourers or *Pannayal*. Education-based economic mobility is seemingly the determinant of this change. The *Mirasdars* who were predominantly Brahmins in the earlier years have now almost completely lost their landholdings. This seems to be due to their increased economic-mobility-driven emigration to the cities. The OBC "neo-elites" have replaced the old order. The result is that the Pallar Pannayal work under the OBC Mirasdars, and one can see an almost complete absence of Brahmins in agriculture today. This marks the changed social reality, because "the correspondence between caste status and class positions has probably diminished over time, where the stratification system has become more open" (Fuller 2012: xx). It must be noted that there are only two Brahmin landowners in the village at present. Neither of them are interested in agriculture. This highlights that "the caste hierarchy and occupational hierarchy are not parallel to one another" (Driver 1982: 228). However, this does not mean that the Brahmins have become economically poor over the years. The *life chances* of the Brahmins are nevertheless "expectantly" better than the Pallar even when their economic status is similar in Sripuram. This is mainly due to the historic reasons that the "lower" the caste the greater the chances of being socio-economically poor in the country. Given their socio-economic dispositions, the erstwhile higher castes are able to secure better life chances.

In this context, one can also observe the increasing irrelevance of land ownership as a central criterion for identifying the poor in the village today. This indicates the need to appreciate the newer forms of social stratification at present. These newer forms can be understood mainly in terms of the intersectionality of the caste, class, gender, education, and employment status of individuals. The caste-based class determinism of social science analysis can therefore be avoided by giving importance to other relevant forms of analysis. In addition, the current ethnographic fieldwork reveals intersectional aspects within the family structure in Sripuram. At present, the relative deprivation of individuals within a family structure is not the same as that of its class position in the village. The disadvantage often goes hand in hand across age, gender, and disability aspects. However, the numerical enumeration of the poor often overlooks the intersectional dynamics (see e.g. Ayres/Simon 2003; Deaton/Dreze 2002; Gang et al. 2004; Jha/Jhingran 2005; Tilak 1999, 2002a, 2002b, 2005, 2007).

In light of this changing economic sphere, the pattern of living as a homogeneous social unit based on caste lines has also begun to shift in Sripuram. This can be contrasted with Beteille's description in which "people belonging to the same group of castes live together, but not necessarily people belonging to the same class" (Beteille 1965: 43). Today, one can however, see the newer pattern of living in the village. This is apparently visible in the *Agraharam*. Although this striking shift has been partly due to the emigration of the Brahmins, one can trace the influences of the broader politico-economic forces that are playing intersectionally from "outside". Increasing economic necessities rearrange livelihoods. It can be argued that neither class nor even caste may *exclusively* constitute a community in future. It is the intersection of various societal factors, this chapter argues, that could play a "deterministic" role in the village.

4 Caste, class, and education

The interrelations between caste, class, and education have brought about significant changes in the social system. These interrelations are *exclusive* in their nature and form for the villagers. The notion of exclusiveness should be observed in light of the primordial identities. For instance, aspects of caste endogamy have to be mentioned. Marital alliances are generally determined according to similarities of caste and class. The final decisions on alliances are often made within the patriarchal family structure.

On a broader level, the role of the state in this social dynamics has been "supportive" of the erstwhile "lower" castes for the political reasons of *votebank*. The notion of votebank, it must be noted, is a sociological concept coined by M. N. Srinivas to define the political class's strategies of treating primordial identities such as caste and the religious factor as a "fixed deposit" with which to win elections in India. Furthermore, it has to be understood in light of the predominant population base of the non-Brahmins on whom the political class depends for its electoral survival in Tamil Nadu. For instance, according to recent demographic figures, nearly 70 per cent of the total population in the state is OBCs and roughly 23 per cent SCs (GoI 2011: 253). In light of this demographic reality in which roughly 93 per cent of the total population is non-Brahmin (which includes both OBCs and SCs), one can find broader policy decisions of a populist nature. This explains the Brahmins' exodus to the "greener economic pastures" of nearby towns. This exodus in Sripuram has to be seen in the absence of economic opportunities and infrastructures that is typical of any village in the country.

The *dominant castes* who have direct socio-economic relationships with the Brahmins, are increasingly emulating the latter in their economic planning today. In this emulation, education is the first domain in which they follow them in their livelihood strategies in Sripuram. The broader political economy often seems to influence the changing nature and forms of caste in the village. This is explicitly visible due to two important policy steps: the anti-untouchability laws and the Reservation policy in the country. Reservation policy in India is often contrasted in line with the affirmative action policies of the United States. However it must be noted that there is a remarkable sociological difference in the nature of discrimination between the caste and racial exclusion in India and the United States. Racial discrimination is most often based on physical appearance such as skin colour. This is in sharp contrast to the caste discrimination that is inclusive of the physical as well as social status. According to the sociological literature on India, individuals are often discriminated even when they are economically well-off if they happen to hail from the lower castes. Because mobility between castes is determined by accidents of birth, the exclusion is a static social factor in the country. As per its affirmative policy, the Indian government reserves a certain percentage of seats in both education and employment for the erstwhile "lower" castes as well as tribes.

While these policy steps are predominantly in support of the erstwhile lower castes, there is unrest as well as livelihood desperation among both orthodox Brahmins and the OBCs in the village. Their perceived marginality due to the protective discrimination policies in both education and employment often makes them, to a large extent, conscious of their caste identity as well as "competitive" in both fields. This competitiveness can be seen in their approach to education. It is most often based on the instrumental ideals for occupational outcome and economic mobility. At conceptual levels, this confirms the ascent of the human capital notion in education. The "competitiveness" under this notion is thus complicated because of its intermeshing with class factors. Because class is not only an economic but also a social category, these complications are often reinforced by education. This has been captured by a "renowned" secular Brahmin in the village called Vishnu. He defines his secular outlook mainly in terms of his detachment from the caste system in the village. In contrast to this detachment, it is important to mention his critique on Reservation:

Due to the Reservation policy, the teaching is mostly being taught by the people who do not have the *knowledge* these days. (*fieldnotes*)

Vishnu, who is known for his "secular" identity in Sripuram, is an intellectually inclined Brahmin individual. His public lectures at the local school celebrations as well as in the nearby villages have earned him a reputation. His opinion on Reservation policy, mentioned above, however, contradicts this reputation. As his critique on this policy resembles that of the orthodox Brahmins, it must be mentioned that a radical opinion such as this cannot be stated in public. This is due to predominant support of the affirmative action policies and the legal implications under the stringent provisions of the anti-untouchability laws.

The presumed priority of caste as the microdeterminant of social contexts suggests how it can be seen working together with class and education in drawing the boundaries that re/produce complex inequalities. In this intersectional social process, there is an urgent need to conceptualize the implications for capability and functionings formation. According to the capability literature, functionings are "the outcomes or achievements, whereas capabilities are the real opportunities to achieve valuable states of being and doing" (Robeyns 2006: 78). The differential outcomes in both capabilities and functionings formations are thus strongly influenced by the intersectionality of caste, class, and education in employment in Sripuram.

In today's modern world in which the changes in the ascriptive division of labour are high, the caste system treats education mainly as an important factor for economic mobility. This is sociologically important, because the social mobility of the castes is relatively difficult when primordial identities are fixed by accidents of birth and, in particular, by the family and caste. In contrast, the structural competition for economic mobility has, however, been under-researched in India. In this context, any mobility analyses have to consider the changing dynamics of individuals' capabilities. For instance, the division of labour is not merely an economic arrangement. The social structure, in contrast to the economic arrangement, most often locates the inheritance based on hereditary affiliations in the village. Although the educational outcome is increasingly changing the landscape of hereditary affiliations mandated mostly by individuals' ascriptive status, the generational failures of the Pallars, for instance, are not allowing them to break the cycle of socio-economic exclusion. Social capital plays a differential role in preserving the status quo in newer forms and nature. This has to be seen in light of the fact that although the social construction of economic success is approached mostly through education, the enabling avenues of informal channels such as the "reference" exert a detrimental influence on the Pallars' agency freedom. With their inferior socio-economic dispositions, Pallars most often have neither the cultural capital nor the habitus. Thus, on the one hand, social mobility is being constrained by the accidents of birth and the systemic issues in educational functionings; on the other hand, these reinforce it in everyday life. Hence, socio-economic mobility and its absence are determined by forces "external" to individuals. These external forces are being influenced by the intersectionality of social factors in Sripuram.

Although the convergence between caste and class continues even today, the educated elite are not drawn mainly from the Brahmins alone who have been historically known for their literate tradition. The functional growth in education, however, does not ensure that diverse caste members will thrive economically in any employable source. The present-day competition and "achievement" initiate a cycle of economic status change but they do not eliminate social inequality. This could be due to the fact that "the principle of equal or equitable distribution, without regard to the recipient's merit, will be an indirect reinforcement of the ascription principle" (Fonseca 1971: 103). Thus, the occupational outcomes of the villagers are shaped mostly by the intersectionality of diverse factors in society. The consequence of this intersectionality often adds complexities to existing socio-economic inequalities. This has to be seen in light of Atal's analysis: "If ascription tends to *perpetu-*

ate the phenomenon of inequality, achievement-orientation *creates* new forms of inequality" (Atal 1971, cited in Fonseca 1971: 92). For instance, the occupational outcome failures of educated un/under-employed youth highlight these newer forms of inequality in Sripuram. The differential outcomes have to been seen differently across the caste–class dynamics (Venkataraman 2013).

Individuals' social capital, as mentioned earlier, often holds the "final" say in their capabilities and functionings in Sripuram. This is despite their personal agency attempts to approach education for economic mobility in the village. The probability of entry into each layer or stage of employment and education has decreased increasingly across the intersectionality of social factors. Against this backdrop, one can say with few exceptions that the lower the class and caste, the higher the chances of being immobile (Venkataraman 2013). Contrary to this, Vishnu's opinion has to be mentioned:

The earlier social order restricted the *Vedic* learnings to the Shudras and manual-learnings to the Brahamanas. But the politicians over the years interpreted it differently. Their interpretations often blamed the Brahmins as the one who prevented the Shudras from education. (*fieldnotes*)

Although such an explanation provides a "convincing" justification to support the orthodox Brahmins, it most often overlooks the fact of opportunity deprivation. The enabling conditions for human flourishing (Nussbaum 2006) are different for the diverse social groups. This can be seen in light of the educated unemployed youths in the village. These youths' inabilities to find adequate opportunities to fulfil the basic economic necessities of life highlight the intersectional implications of their capability deprivations. Against this backdrop, the Brahmins, irrespective of their class position, have been competing well with their peers in the system. This is mostly due to their realization that economic mobility can be reached mainly through education. This is in line with their socio-economic position in which there is a class-based difference in the kinds of schools they attend. The educational reality in Sripuram is somewhat similar to the common arguments that the "social classes differ considerably in years of schooling" (Driver 1982: 232). Although one can see the class differences in the type of schools individuals attend, the striking fact is the increasing continuation of education across the diverse social groups in the village. The qualification of escalation or the degrees without any *real* freedom can be a reason for the functionings failure, but the agency's sustained educational engagements to a smaller extent provides them the opportunity to reflect on their available choices in life. Thus, to reiterate the class differences in educational attainment, it must be mentioned that in light of the quality predicaments:

Without a significant commitment by the state to improve the quality and reach of government education, a dual-track education system in which traditionally excluded castes and classes are only able to access the lowest quality education opportunities may become a permanent feature of the Indian education system aggravating socio-economic inequality. The community "has been unable to prevent the decline in the quality of schooling". (Hill et al. 2011: 105)

Thus, as in other parts of the country, the local school in Sripuram, for instance, is largely segregated on the basis of class positions. The fee-demanding "quality" private education institutions are most often the "preferred" destination of the non-poor. The economically poor, in contrast, are mostly seen in the fee-free local school in the village. However, the fee-free school, like any other government institution, is notorious for its low-quality services. This can be seen in the inferior teaching-learning processes and other systemic variables. Along these systemic variables, the intersectional social factors of caste and class in education reinforce the functionings' failures, and this, in turn, ensures capability deprivation. The consequence can be seen in terms of the interplay of diverse factors both in terms of systemic issues as well as structural factors in systematically ensuring these failures in the village. The intersectional process of caste and class dynamics, on the one hand, is making education a tool in the re/production of an unequal social order. The systemic limitations of quality, on the other hand, ensure weak conversion factors. This altogether underscores the complexities of capability deprivation.

Against this backdrop, the villagers irrespective of their financial burdens, are increasingly interested in sending their children to fee-paying private schools. This could be due to their *adaptive preferences* to search of an educational outcome. Although their desperate search for quality in education for their wards could be due to their agency rationality, it can be seen in light of human capital ideals. The agency rationality is seemingly being exploited by private education providers. The non-poor across all the castes in Sripuram, for instance, often compete for the same "quality" institutions in Meenakshipuram.[8] The rising education "demand" encourages private schools to keep increasing their fees. This once again systematically excludes the poor due to their inability to pay. Individuals' financial inability, at times, can be seen in their re-entry to the local school in the village. If they happen to be from the Pallar (which is most often the case), the structural factors of intersectionality push them even further towards the educational periphery. Consequently, they are deprived of the conversion factors that will enhance their capabilities and functionings. The competitive approach to education by the non-poor, who are mostly from castes other than the Pallars of Sripuram, not

---

8   Meenakshipuram is a pseudonymously named small town nearest to Sripuram. This is one of the Block headquarters in Tanjore district.

only re/produces but also reinforces the "status summation" in society. This points to the importance of intersectionality in which the discussion on caste, class, and education provides a useful starting point when accounting for social change. This change, in the present context, underlines the declining rural character of Sripuram where education is one of the primary intersectional factors.

5   Conclusion

In India, the socio-economically backward groups are conceived mainly as the Scheduled Castes (SCs) and Scheduled Tribes (STs). Although the notion of backwardness is largely established, the complexity of social stratification needs to be appreciated. This appreciation is critical when the ascriptive status can no longer command the same economic influence as it had in earlier years. This is why one can see marginal individuals even in "higher" castes today. Although this is most often economic in nature, the interplay of various factors discussed in the preceding sections has to be comprehended in order to capture the complex social realities such as that of Sripuram. The disaggregations of this complexity have been seen in intersectionality. The cumulative effects of socio-economic factors present in the village set the ethnographic basis for adopting intersectional analyses. This has allowed the author to look at the issues in totality instead of empirical "reductionisms".

In today's India, the qualities of opportunities are thus, generally determined by intersectional social forces. These forces are predominantly shaped by the identities of caste, class, and family. The discussion on intersectional analysis is crucial, because mobility can no longer be viewed as a phenomenon of movement of individuals only on the basis of the ascriptive considerations of caste. There is an urgent need to study the niceties of intersectional factors and the availabilities of resources for socializing the next generation. This urgency has to be seen in terms of the role of intersectionality in reinforcing its influence on recruitments *even* in the informal economies of village India. In addition, it must also be noted that the inequalities of opportunity of the erstwhile "lower" castes are expectantly lower, given their historical exclusion from society. As this has been well-established in academia (see e.g. Breman 2004; Gorringe et al. 2009), it is high time to leave the poor and marginalized from the persistent exploitation 'at least' in research. The need of the hour could be to study the mobility trajectories of the "upper" social stratum in the country. This is essential for broader theory building. This could be a possible research direction for future studies taking the intersectional perspective.

Theorization, it must be reiterated, is one of the important mandates of academia instead of continuously reinventing the same old wheels about the poor and the marginalized. In light of this, sociologists can also counter the economic determinism in India. For instance, if qualitative studies take up the issue of the intersectional employment history of the parent(s), it could certainly be a valuable addition on the conceptual levels. This will possibly allow academics to theorize on the matrices of mobility. Both sociological and ethnographic research, for instance, can make use of the insightful inferences on intergenerational mobility to be found in their sustained "field" observations. This is conceptually essential, given the statistical limitations in which it is astonishing to see that even the National Sample Survey (NSS) is under-sampling the rich. As this is also visible in mainstream academia, the consequence is that measures understate the actual degree of inequality in income in India (Weisskopf 2011: 45).

Thus, an emphasis in status-attainment research on the "higher" castes and classes will certainly show how individual agencies are being shaped by the intersectional forces in India today. Against this backdrop, another probable research direction could be to understand how the non-poor, who are most often being represented in the erstwhile "higher" castes, are currently cultivating their children's talents and abilities. This is important, because these are the functional conversion factors for broader capability and functionings formations (Sen 1999). Analyses of this nature will also lead us to understand both micro as well as macro social processes through which the family of origin re/produces the well-being of the non-poor and the "higher" castes in later life.

This is important in India because mainstream research has so far been unable to counter the inconvenient "truths" in the country. For instance, there is no conceptual scrutiny of why the educationists' "personally" prefer to send their own children to private schools despite their "professional" opposition to the privatization of education in India. These inconvenient intersectional truths are crucial to understand how the policy elites are convinced by market principles despite "strong" academic opposition. This may well be due to their "awareness" of the personal *choices* and professional *voices* of today's academics.

References

Ayres, Ron/Torrijos Simon, Manuela (2003): Education, Poverty and Sustainable Livelihoods in Tamil Nadu: Inequalities, Opportunities and Constraints. In: Review of Political Economy, 15, 2, pp. 211–229.

Beteille, Andre (1965): Caste, Class and Power: Changing Patterns of Stratification in a Tanjore Village. New Delhi: Oxford University Press.
Breman, Jan (2004): Return of Social Inequality: A Fashionable Doctrine. In: Economic and Political Weekly, 39, 35, pp. 3869–3872.
Choo, Hae Yeon/Ferree, Myra Marx (2010): Practicing Intersectionality in Sociological Research: A Critical Analysis of Inclusions, Interactions, and Institutions in the Study of Inequalities. In: Sociological Theory, 28, 2, pp. 129–149.
D' Souza, Victor S. (1999): Review of "Caste, Class, and Power: Changing Patterns of Stratification in a Tanjore Village" by Andre Beteille. In: Sociological Bulletin, 48, 1 & 2, pp. 298–302.
Deaton, Angus/Dreze, Jean Dreze (2002): Poverty and Inequality in India: A Re-Examination. In: Economic and Political Weekly, September 7, pp. 3729–3748.
Deliege, Robert (2011): Caste, Class and Untouchability. In: Clark-Deces, Isabelle (ed.): A Companion to the Anthropology of India. West Sussex: Wiley-Blackwell, UK. pp. 45–61.
Driver, Edwin D. (1982): Class, caste, and 'status summation' in urban South India. In: Contributions to Indian Sociology, 16, 2, pp. 225–253.
Fonseca, Aloysius J. (ed.) (1971): Challenge of Poverty in India. Delhi: Vikas Publications.
Fuller, Christopher J. (2012): New Introduction to "Caste, Class and Power". In: Beteille, Andre: Caste, Class and Power. New Delhi: Oxford University Press (2nd Edition/Sixth Impression) [Oxford India Perennials 2012].
Gang, Ira N./Sen, Kunal/Yun, Myeong-Su (2004): Caste, Ethnicity and Poverty in Rural India. In: Institute for the Study of Labor (IZA), Research Paper Series, November 27.
Gorringe, Hugo/Jeffery, Roger/Sariola, Salla (2009): Ethnographic Insights into Enduring Inequalities. In: Journal of South Asian Development, 4, 1, pp. 1–6.
Government of India (GoI) (2011): India Human Development Report 2011: Towards Social Inclusion. New Delhi: Oxford University Press.
Hill, Elizabeth/Samson, Meera/Dasgupta, Shyamasree (2011): Expanding the School Market in India: Parental Choice and the Reproduction of Social Inequality. In: Economic and Political Weekly, XLVI, 35, pp. 98–105.
Jha, Jyotsna/Jhingran, Dhir (2005): Elementary Education for the Poorest and other Deprived Groups: The Real Challenge of Universalization. New Delhi: Manohar Publishers.
Mencher, Joan P. (1970): A Tamil Village: Changing Socioeconomic Structure in Madras State. In: Ishwaran, K. (ed.): Change and Continuity in India's Villages. New York: Columbia University Press, pp. 197–218.
Nandy, Santosh Kumar (1966): Review of "Caste, Class, and Power: Changing Patterns of Stratification in a Tanjore Village" by Andre Beteille. In: American Sociological Review, 31, 5, pp. 729–730.
Nussbaum, Martha (2006): Education and Democratic Citizenship: Capabilities and Quality Education. In: Journal of Human Development, 7, 3, pp. 385–395.
Robeyns, Ingrid (2006): Three Models of education: Rights, capabilities and human capital. In: Theory and Research in Education, 4, 1, pp. 69–84.
Sen, Amartya (1999): Development as Freedom. New Delhi: Oxford University Press.
Shields, Stephanie A. (2008): Gender: An Intersectionality Perspective. In: Sex Roles, 59, 5–6, pp. 301–311.

Srinivas, M N (1987): The Dominant Caste and Other Essays. New Delhi: Oxford University Press.
Tilak, Jandhyala BG (1999): Education and Poverty in South Asia. In: Prospects: Quarterly Review of Comparative Education, XXIX, 4, pp. 517–533.
Tilak, Jandhyala BG (2002a): Education and Poverty. In: Journal of Human Development, 3, 2, pp. 191–207.
Tilak, Jandhyala BG (2002b): Education poverty in India. In: Review of Development and Change, VII, 1, pp. 1–44.
Tilak, Jandhyala BG (2005): Post-Elementary Education, Poverty and Development in India. Paper presented on 8th UKFIET Oxford International Conference on Education and Development: Learning and Livelihoods (13–15th September 2005), University of Oxford, UK (unpublished).
Tilak, Jandhyala BG (2007): Post-elementary education, poverty and development in India. In: International Journal of Educational Development, 27, pp. 435–445.
Venkataraman, Lakshmi N. (2013): Quality, employability and capabilities: The enduring elusive triangle in Indian education. In: ASIEN: The German Journal on Contemporary Asia, 127, pp. 30–47.
Weisskopf, Thomas E. (2011): Why Worry about Inequality in the Booming Indian Economy? In: Economic and Political Weekly, XLVI, 47, pp. 41–51.

Capabilities of Young People

Franziska Eisenhuth

Refugee Children in Germany: Acting Within a Framework of Capability Constraints

1 Basic considerations: Refugees as "margizens" in receiving countries

Refugees are a group that is outstandingly vulnerable to marginalisation. Their vulnerability does not disappear once they have fled from their countries of origin. Instead, in receiving countries, "margizens", as Martiniello (1994: 41f.) calls them referring to the case of EU countries, enjoy only extremely limited civil, socio-economic, and political rights or even – in the case of so-called illegal or undocumented immigrants – almost no rights at all.

Hence, as long as refugees have not gained a permanent resident status in an EU member state, they in no way have the same life chances as other inhabitants. In fact, Martiniello (1994: 41f.) argues that non-EU citizens without a permanent resident status in an EU country are placed at the bottom of a system of civic stratification.

The term margizen indicates that their underprivileged status is the result of marginalisation, namely, of a systematic structural discrimination based on differentiated laws. Therefore, this term seems to be more appropriate to describe people without a permanent resident status than the term "displaced persons" used in official EU documents. The idea that these persons originally belong to another place from which they are displaced casts some light on the nationalist logic followed by EU legislation (see Martiniello 1994: 42), and it focuses on their former lives in their countries of origin, whereas the term margizen points to their current marginalisation in receiving countries.

Martiniello's work dates back to the early 1990s. When describing the current situation of non-citizens in receiving countries, it is often stated that migrants' rights have improved (see Mohr 2005: 383). But the situation is more complicated as Katrin Mohr notes in her analysis of Britain and Germany:

> We can see that some migrant groups are facing contractions of their rights and that economic restructuring, welfare state retrenchment, and socio-economic marginality are lead-

ing to the erosion of social rights even of long-term residents and their offspring. (Mohr 2005: 383)

In the case of margizens, Mohr shows that their rights have become even been more restricted in the 2000s. Mohr's comment also points out that the marginalisation of migrants cannot be reduced to the restriction of their rights. It goes even further when rights on paper are not being realised due to other limitations. Mohr refers to "socio-economic marginality" (see above) that de facto puts margizens in a weak position when it comes to exercising the rights they do have. But one should also mention other aspects, especially everyday racism, that lead to discrimination against margizens in, for example, the allocation of jobs or housing (see e.g. Feagin/McKinney 2003).

Hence, margizens remain vulnerable in receiving countries due not only to their underprivileged position in a system of civic stratification but also further limitations interwoven with their legal discrimination.

Proceeding from these remarks, this chapter argues for a justice-based or, more concretely a capabilities perspective on margizens. Martha Nussbaum's capabilities approach is regarded as a useful evaluative framework for their situation in receiving countries (2.1). Among the heterogeneous group of margizens, refugee children are especially vulnerable due to their dependency on others and to intergenerational power structures (2.2). Their marginalisation is perpetuated by their widespread and far-reaching under-representation in research within the social sciences.

This chapter reports on a qualitative study focusing on their situation (3.). Its results reveal various and partly severe capability constraints on the children (3.1) but also show the children's different strategies for acting within this framework (3.2). Hence, it is argued that the combination of the capabilities approach with a decentred idea of agency from childhood studies leads to a mutual enrichment when observing the situation of refugee children (4.).

2 Theoretical considerations

2.1 Margizens from a capabilities perspective

The comments on the discrimination of margizens in receiving countries indicate the value of discussing this topic from a justice-based perspective and, more concretely, from a capabilities perspective. If everybody should have the equal right "to choose a life one has reason to value" (Sen 1999: 74), the legal and social situation of margizens in receiving countries has to be examined critically. Their exclusion from rights has to be questioned, because it massively restricts their possibilities to choose their ways of life.

With a capabilities perspective, it is possible to go beyond the analysis of rights on paper but also point to further restrictions of free choice. Martha Nussbaum states that "liberty is not just a matter of having rights on paper, it requires being in a position to exercise those rights. And this requires material and institutional resources" (Nussbaum 2000: 54).

Moreover, the capabilities approach according to Martha Nussbaum can provide a normative framework for the detailed analysis of the life situations of margizens. Nussbaum's list of ten central human capabilities (see Nussbaum 2007: 76f.) functions as an approximate operationalisation of human dignity. Nussbaum proposes central life chances that should be granted to all human beings in order to enable them to live a valuable life according to their own values. Thus, this list also gives hints regarding which specific life chances margizens should have but do not actually have.

Referring to Martha Nussbaum's list of capabilities, it can be argued that, for instance, the capability of control over one's environment is being harmed because margizens do not enjoy political rights in Germany. Martha Nussbaum states that this capability entails "being able to participate effectively in political choices that govern one's life; having the right of political participation, protections of free speech and association" (Nussbaum 2007: 77).

There are many more feasible links to Nussbaum's list of capabilities. An analysis of the German[1] Asylum Seekers' Benefit Act (*Asylbewerberleistungsgesetz* [AsylbLG]) can be used to illustrate this idea. This law has been governing social benefits for asylum seekers and people with a "temporary suspension of deportation" (*Duldung*)[2] in Germany for almost 20 years. In different regions of Germany, these people receive no cash payments (except for a small amount of "pocket money") but food and clothing vouchers or food packets that leave extremely little or no choice at all regarding what they eat and wear. This treatment is unique in Germany; no other social group receives social benefit in this way.

From a capabilities perspective, it can be argued that these regulations restrict the possibilities of margizens to live a decent life. For instance, their capability of bodily health is being harmed, because they often receive food packets containing canned goods and no fresh fruit or vegetables. Therefore, it can be argued that they have no access to adequate nutrition, an aspect of

---

1 Because the study referred to in this chapter was conducted in Germany, the German situation will be focused in detail even though, also due to so-called EU harmonisation, there are obvious parallels to the situations in other receiving EU countries as Martiniello's (1994) and Mohr's (2005) work has already shown.

2 Asylum seekers receive a "Duldung" if their application for asylum has been rejected but they cannot be deported from Germany because of, for example, the security situation in their country of origin, their being unable to travel, or their having no passport. As soon as their deportation is possible, they have to leave Germany (§60 a AufenthG).

the capability of bodily health. But also if margizens are given vouchers, their possibilities to choose healthy food are restricted because of the low level of social benefit they receive: fruit and vegetables are more expensive and less nutritious than instant meal products.

Further capabilities are at stake, for example, because margizens are in danger of becoming victims of racist attacks in Germany, thereby hurting the capability of bodily integrity: "being able to move freely from place to place; to be secure against violent assault" (Nussbaum 2007: 76), and hurting the capability of affiliation by threatening the "social bases of self-respect and non-humiliation" (Nussbaum 2007: 77).

However, one aspect should be mentioned if Nussbaum's approach is to be adapted to the situation of margizens. As Nivedita Menon (2002) points out, Nussbaum strongly affirms national states as the units responsible for distributing justice. In her book "Frontiers of justice" (Nussbaum 2007), she even expresses a "moral belief that one should respect the sovereignty of any nation that is organized in a sufficiently accountable way, whether or not its institutions are fully just" (Nussbaum 2007: 256). This belief is based on her idea that the national state "is the largest and most foundational unit that still has any chance of being decently accountable to the people who live there" (Nussbaum 2007: 257).

Following Nancy Fraser (2008), this argumentation should be questioned, because viewing existing national states as the only units within which justice applies drastically limits, if not wholly excludes, transnational obligations of justice (see Fraser 2008: 55). If the nation state is deemed as the unit in charge of distributing justice, it also becomes difficult to analyse the violence implied in nationalist demarcations that are constitutive for national states such as the system of civic stratification with its implied hierarchy of rights, as Martiniello (1994) shows.

Nevertheless, Nussbaum also describes it as her aim to extend

> justice to all world citizens, showing theoretically how we might realize a world that is just as a whole, in which accidents of birth and national origin do not warp people's life chances pervasively and from the start. (Nussbaum 2007: 2)

Following this idea, this chapter aims to criticise an aspect of transnational inequality from a capabilities perspective even though it does not share Nussbaum's belief in the benefit of national states. However, the capabilities approach is used because it underpins the critique of the structural discrimination of margizens from a sound justice-based perspective.

2.2 Social justice for refugee children

This chapter focuses on a special subgroup within the heterogeneous group of margizens: on children. The Office of the UNHCR (United Nations High Commissioner for Refugees) states: "Almost half of the world's forcibly displaced people are children."[3] (UNHCR n.d.) This includes children who have had to escape from their countries of origin as well as children whose parents fled and who themselves were born in a receiving country.

It is not just the high number of refugee children all over the world that makes their situation deserving of special interest. Childhood is also a life stage with a special vulnerability, because children are only gradually developing in terms of, for example, their abilities, their likings, and their autonomy. As long as they are young, and also the younger they are, the more they are dependent on others to support these processes of development. Hence, they rely on people who will help them to develop their own ways of life, as indicated in the UN Convention on the Rights of the Child (UN General Assembly 1989).[4]

Whereas it is important to point to this special vulnerability of children, there is, at the same time, the danger of essentialising children's vulnerability: The idea that children are especially vulnerable is also a source to oppress them, as Alan Prout (2000: 10) points out.

Whilst children, like many others, may at times be vulnerable, there is a push towards its use as a master identity for children. Ideologically children are separated from adults, rendered as objects of concern, help and intervention, and minimized in their capacity for dealing with their problems. At the same time their actual experiences, those that they experience as vulnerability, are not much listened to by adults.

This indicates that children's vulnerability is also caused by intergenerational power structures. That is why they have to be protected from exploitation – another aspect emphasized in the UN Convention on the Rights of the Child (UN General Assembly 1989).

For the special case of refugee children, I would like to argue that it is important to examine at least two "governance structures" (Fraser 2008). First, a system of civic stratification substantially restricts margizens' rights whilst further limiting their possibilities to choose a life they have reason to value because they cannot wholly exercise the rights they do have on paper.

---

3   It is further specified here that "forcibly displaced people" means "refugees, internally displaced, asylum-seekers or stateless" (UNHCR n.d.). In my understanding, children with temporary resident permits as well as children without any resident permits should also be included as refugee children. This would significantly increase the size of this group.
4   The convention includes the idea that every child has the right of "full and harmonious development of his or her personality" (UN General Assembly 1989: preamble).

Second, margizens who are children are further marginalised by their dependency on others and by intergenerational power structures.[5]

It is therefore crucial to pay special attention to the question of justice for refugee children. But within capabilities debates, there seems to be a broad consensus that children in general are not autonomous enough to be taken into account as capable agents. That is why they are mostly not deemed to be entitled to freely choose the lives they have reason to value. Nevertheless, it seems crucial to include children in a capabilities perspective on justice in order to reduce intergenerational inequality. Theoretically, this is possible if autonomy is being analysed critically as an ideal benchmark that adults also fail to reach in every situation (Clark/Eisenhuth 2011). Martha Nussbaum (2007: 87f.) also argues that it is constitutive for human beings to be dependent on others to different extents during their lifespan. If autonomy is recognised more selectively, children can be included as equal addressees of social justice in a capabilities perspective (see Clark/Eisenhuth 2011, for a more detailed argumentation).

3 The study: Refugee children in Germany

The marginalisation of refugee children is perpetuated by their serious under-representation in research from a social-science perspective. As Dawn Chatty et al. (2012: 387) point out, until recently, most research on refugees has been carried out on adults. Studies including children are located mostly in the domains of psychology and psychiatry and tend to pathologise their research subjects. Thus, research on refugee children based on a justice-based perspective can make a productive contribution to closing this research gap.

Following this idea, the life situations of refugee children in Germany were examined in a qualitative interview-based study. Twelve interviews with primary-school-aged refugee children in Germany were carried out from May 2009 to May 2010. Out of this sample, six interviews (ranging in length from 45 minutes to 2 hours) were chosen for in-depth analyses and related to a capabilities perspective.

The research interest of this project can be further specified by two sets of questions. First, it asks which capabilities refugee children do or do not have in Germany. To get to the core of this main question, the following research questions were developed:

5 Of course, other governance structures are also relevant from an intersectional perspective, as, for example, Allison James (2009: 44) points out when she argues that "childhood is fragmented by social variables such as class, gender, ethnicity and health status". Nonetheless, this chapter narrows the focus to two governance structures in order to analyse one aspect of social inequality in more detail.

- Which possibilities do refugee children have to develop their full human potential?
- Which decisions are they able to take?
- Which goods and resources do they dispose of?
- Which aspects restrict their agency?

The first question explicitly asks for the capabilities of the children. Here, my understanding of "full human potential" is inspired by Martha Nussbaum's list of capabilities. The second question on the decisions they are able or not able to take also points to the capabilities they do or do not possess. The third question addresses the material conditions for realising capabilities, whereas the fourth question focuses on aspects that restrict this realisation.

However, the research project goes beyond a mere orientation towards Nussbaum's list of capabilities and also focuses on refugee children's perspectives on their own life situations. Instead of essentialising their vulnerability, this views them as subjects whose perspectives on their own living conditions are relevant. The following questions were asked:

- What do refugee children deem important in their lives?
- Which perspectives do they have on their own living conditions?
- Which wishes and aspirations do they have?

By combining these two sets of questions, the aim was to address an aspect of social inequality through two different perspectives – through a capabilities perspective and through the eyes of the ones who are subjected to margizen- and child-specific governance structures.

The interviews were analysed on the basis of the Grounded Theory research strategy as outlined by Barney Glaser and Anselm Strauss (1979) and further developed by Anselm Strauss and Juliet Corbin (2008). The data were initially examined in an open coding process (by "asking questions, making comparisons, throwing out ideas, and brainstorming"; Strauss/Corbin 2008: 169f.). Then, those codes that appeared to be relevant to the research questions were grouped into concepts (as "words that stand for ideas contained in the data"; see Strauss/Corbin 2008: 159) and categories (as "higher-level concepts" that represent relevant phenomena; Strauss/Corbin 2008: 159).

The analysis of the children's utterances from a capabilities perspective revealed different constraints that make it difficult for these children to live the lives they have reason to value. But they also show the children's different strategies for acting in a framework of constraints.

3.1 Results: Capability constraints

The analyses of the interviews revealed that the constraints faced by refugee children in Germany can be grouped into the following three different aspects (or "categories" in Grounded Theory terminology):

a. Restricted possibilities of shaping their living environment
b. Ethnic difference
c. Threatened future

The following describes these three different aspects in more detail and relates them to the lack of different capabilities. It will be argued that the interaction of these three aspects results in a marginalisation that has to be considered to be specific to refugee children in Germany.

3.1.1 Capability constraints – Restricted possibilities of shaping their living environment

First, the analyses of the interviews reveal what are in part severe restrictions to refugee children's mobility, consumption, and housing conditions. These three topics (or "concepts" in Grounded Theory terminology) can be described as aspects of possibilities to shape their own living environments.

The following examples illustrate the nature of these constraints, first focusing on mobility:

Nine-year-old Leotrim lives 15 km away from his best friend, because Leotrim's family moved to another town. Now Leotrim cannot see his friend anymore. He reports that the reason for this is that his father cannot obtain a driving license because the obligatory driving lessons are too expensive for the family. There is also no efficient local transport system. Therefore, this restriction of Leotrim's mobility is caused by his family's poverty and a lack of public infrastructure.

Ten-year-old Edon reports that he cannot visit his grandfather in Norway although he is seriously sick and could die at any time. This is because Edon's family has a *"Duldung"* (see above), which means that they are not even allowed to leave the German administrative district they are living in, let alone the country (AsylVfG §56).

The two examples show that both children are clearly limited in their possibilities to maintain their social relationships due to the restriction to their mobility that, in Leotrim's case, is related to poverty; in Edon's case, to his family's status as margizens. In both cases, it can be argued that the capability of emotions is being violated (see Nussbaum 2007: 76f.) because it is hard for the boys to be attached to family and friends if they are unable to visit them however much they may miss them.

The analyses of the interviews reveal not only constraints to mobility but also to consumption and housing conditions that are caused directly by margizens' regimentation through specific laws (such as the movement restriction, AsylVfG §56, in Edon's case) and by refugee children's poverty (as Leotrim's example shows).

At the same time, however, the children's poverty also has to be understood as being related to their status as margizens. The families of four out of the six children whose interviews are analysed here were living from social benefits as specified in the Asylum Seekers' Benefit Act (*Asylbewerberleistungsgesetz*). As a result, they had extremely little money at their disposal. Some of the children's fathers had no work permit and therefore no legal chance to earn more money for their family. The ones who did earn money were working under precarious conditions and had no fixed and secure income. None of the mothers of the interviewed children had any income. In this context, it has to be mentioned that every job in Germany has to be offered to German nationals first, then to other EU citizens, followed by to non-EU citizens with a secure residence status, before finally becoming available to a margizen (AufenthG §39 [2]). As a result, only the most unattractive jobs are left for margizens.

These remarks show that distinguishing constraints related to insecure residence status from those related to poverty is actually of only limited use. Concerning consumption, this can be illustrated by the example of 11-year-old Selcan who is very interested in music and can play the flute and the guitar. She would like to learn to play the piano as well, but her family has no chance to satisfy her wish because of their poverty. Although there may be many families – both margizens and others – who cannot afford piano lessons, and even more who cannot afford a piano, for Selcan's family, it is virtually impossible to pay for piano lessons because they only receive a small amount of "pocket money" and otherwise receive food and clothing vouchers in line with the Asylum Seekers' Benefit Act (*Asylbewerberleistungsgesetz*). Therefore, the possibility of buying goods of their own choice is extremely limited, and, as a result, Selcan's freedom to choose leisure activities she values is restricted as well.

Selcan's case points to the ways in which constraints in consumption limit refugee children's possibilities to realise their wishes for self-realisation and thereby cut down the capability of senses, imagination, and thought (see Nussbaum 2007: 76) and the capability of play (see Nussbaum 2007: 77).

3.1.2 Capability constraints – Ethnic difference

The second set of capability constraints lies on a symbolic level. It is revealed in the fact that the refugee children who were interviewed describe themselves and their families as being different in various aspects – different, as the analyses show, from Germans, even though they do not make this explicit. More concretely, the children describe their own "different origin", "different religion", and "language difference" – the relevant concepts that group together to form the category of ethnic difference. The three concepts can be seen as different manifestations of the same phenomenon, because all of them can be understood as aspects of ethnicity.

An example for this is 7-year-old Muna's answer when asked whether she liked the town she is living in. Muna says that she likes it here because in her "old home country", as she puts it, there was a war. So even though she is not being asked about the country she comes from, Muna links a question about her present life situation to her origin. In reaction, she explains the war in her "old home country" is the reason why she is in Germany, which might be her "new home country" now.

This case can be connected to dominant discourses in Germany that emphasize the importance of ethnicity: People who have not been born in Germany ("different origin"), who are not Christian ("different religion"), and/or speak another language than German or do not speak German correctly (both aspects of "language difference" as revealed in the interviews) are imagined to deviate from an imagined German community (see Anderson 1985). Consequently, discourses of ethnic difference also lead to symbolic exclusions of refugee children from a German collective.

Through the attribution of ethnic difference, the capabilities of refugee children are constrained in a subtle way. For these children, the possibilities to present themselves are restricted symbolically. In everyday situations, they have to explain their difference and legitimise being in Germany, as Muna also does in the interview situation. In extreme cases, when ethnic difference is used explicitly to devaluate refugee children, they are insulted in a racist way. Both Edon and Leotrim reported incidents in which their teacher told them to go back to Kosovo (Edon) or even insulted them as "f****ing foreigners" (Leotrim). They also stated that this behaviour had no negative consequences for their teacher.

Therefore, in addition to their restricted possibilities of shaping their own living environments, refugee children are restricted on a symbolic level. I would like to argue that the capability of affiliation (see Nussbaum 2007: 77) is at stake here, because children are, more or less subtly, being excluded from a German community because of their perceived ethnic difference. This becomes very clear when they are openly humiliated by being exposed to racist insults.

3.1.3 Capability constraints – Threatened future

The third aspect of capability constraints for refugee children deals with the fact that it is impossible to make concrete plans for their future and they have to fear being deported from Germany. This is especially apparent in the case of 8-year-old Adnan who explicitly describes this fear in detail, telling that he is so afraid that the people who are going to deport him and his family will come at night when he is sleeping. He has no personal connection to Turkey, the country he would be deported to, he does not know anybody there, and he does not speak Turkish. The existential threat of being deported also completely prevents Adnan from talking about his future life and makes it very difficult for him to express any wish that is not connected to this aspect.

Hence, a future threatened in this way imposes at least two restrictions on refugee children: on the one hand, their possibilities to plan their lives are limited; on the other hand, their current living situations are severely constrained when the existential fear of being deported decreases the quality of their lives. From a capabilities perspective, it is reasonable to say that the capability of practical reason that should ensure the possibility to actively plan one's own life is being harmed (see Nussbaum 2007: 77). Also the capability of emotions is influenced by anxiety (see Nussbaum 2007: 76f.).

Summing up the case of refugee children in Germany, different capability constraints limit their possibilities to live the lives they have reason to value. These constraints mutually support each other: Dominant discourses that exclude margizens from an imagined German community symbolically (see "ethnic difference") sustain their exclusion from rights that then leads, in turn, to a lack of resources (see "restricted possibilities of shaping their living environment") and to existential threats regarding their situation in Germany (see "threatened future"). Their marginalised legal status reconfirms discourses of exclusion. The outcome of the intertwining of the three aspects shown here is a material and symbolic exclusion that has to be considered to be specific for the living situations of refugee children in Germany.

3.2 Results: Capability constraints and agency

Even though the capability constraints that refugee children have to face are severe and partly even existential, recognising this does not mean that these children should be viewed as passive objects of oppression. This idea would foster their victimisation and perpetuate their marginalisation.

Instead, as indicated above, refugee children should be understood as subjects who are embedded in structures of capability constraints, but who also exercise agency within this framework. Agency is understood against the background of a direction within childhood studies taken particularly by Allison James and Alan Prout. For these authors,

> Children are and must be seen as active in the construction and determination of their own social lives, the lives of those around them and of the societies in which they live. Children are not just the passive subjects of social structures and processes. (James/Prout 2007: 8)

These authors' perspective has been widely criticised for essentialising children's agency and thereby losing sight of the fact that children's possibilities to determine their own lives and living environments are clearly limited by structural constraints – as the results of the present study illustrate for the case of refugee children. In this way, the critique points to the need to conceptualise children's agency in a differentiated way, or to "decentre agency" (Prout 2000: 16), as Alan Prout puts it.

In fact, already in their earlier work, James and Prout suggested the need to "address both structure and agency in the same movement" (James/Prout 1995: 81); that is, to also always see a child as "both an effect and a cause of the environments within which they engage" (James/Prout 1995: 89). Following these assumptions, refugee children – as all children and as all subjects – should be deemed as agents whose actions are limited by structural constraints but who still "bring about some effect" in the structures in which they are embedded (see Prout 2000: 16).

Empirically, refugee children's agency can be discovered in the various ways in which they deal with the capability constraints presented above. This assumption will be illustrated by some examples:

Eight-year-old Idris, for instance, criticises the living conditions of his family, especially because they have no garden. But he also protests that his family disposes of insufficient money, that he lacks specific toys he would like to have, that his mobility is restricted, and that, as a result, he is often bored. Basically, Idris would just like to live like the other children he knows. Indeed, he criticises all aspects of the restricted possibilities to shape one's living environments that have been found in the interviews (housing conditions, consumption, and mobility).

His explicit critique is thereby deemed to be a way for Idris to position himself against the capability constraints he experiences and is therefore seen as a way to perform agency. Idris' critique will not improve his materially deprived situation, but it is a strategy to actively engage with it.

The interview with Leotrim reveals a quite contrary way of engaging with poverty: When he was asked what a perfect future would look like for him, Leotrim reported that he would like to live "in a completely normal way". Furthermore, it would be nice if his family could be living next to Leotrim's uncle, but the most important thing is to have an apartment anyway.

So Leotrim explicitly refers to a "normal life" – as Idris implicitly does. But the children seem to have different conceptions of this normality. Instead of expressing desires for material goods such as toys as Idris does, or also wishing for immaterial goods such as health as the other children do, Leotrim does not strive for big changes. His family already lives in an apartment with about 70 m² (about 750 ft²) of living space and four rooms for seven people. Compared to German standards, this is not much space. In the town that Leotrim is living in, the social welfare office for instance would define a flat of 105 m² (about 1,130 ft²) as "adequate" for a family the size of Leotrim's. But when Leotrim is asked how he likes this apartment, he says that he likes it very much, and that four rooms are enough. It is as if he anticipates that the interviewer will implicitly criticise the size of the apartment. This example indicates that living conditions, which can be described as materially deprived in comparison to local standards, can be accepted and integrated into a positive perspective on the children's own living conditions.

Empirically, a hint to this acceptance can be found in the cases of those children who place special emphasis on their families and/or their friends. That does not mean that the children who criticise their own material deprivation do not value their social relationships. All children who were interviewed described their friends or family as important in one or the other way, but some of them mentioned their importance often and without being asked.

Against this background, it seems reasonable to understand the special, intrinsic importance of social relationships as a factor that fosters a certain acceptance of material deprivation – at least if it is assumed that not mentioning poverty is a hint of acceptance. In this way, social relationships may soften the experiences of constraints for some children and enable them to present themselves as satisfied with their living situations.

So describing one's own living situation as satisfying, as Leotrim does, is quite contrary to the critique Idris utters, but it is seen as a way to perform agency as well. Taking material deprivation for granted and integrating it into a positive perspective on his own life enables Leotrim to say that he is satisfied. He thereby actively engages with his own life situation and sees it in a positive light.

It has to be mentioned that the present study did not aim to attribute specific ways of performing agency to the individual children who were interviewed, stating that, for example, Idris shows a way of criticising capability constraints whereas Leotrim accepts them. Instead, it shows empirically that the individual children reveal different performances of agency, for example, integrating a part of capability limitations into a positive perspective whilst criticising another aspect.

Thus, Leotrim, without being asked, says that he wants to stay in Germany because this is where his friends are and because he was born here – a hint on the fact that many margizens live in Germany for many years without ever gaining a permanent resident status. Adnan and Edon also state that they want to stay in Germany because it is the centre of their lives.

Here, the children reject dominant discourses that exclude refugee children from Germany and symbolically place them in other countries. Their arguments on why they want to stay in Germany can also be seen as an aspect of their agency; and, at the same time, this way of exercising agency is clearly limited, because they are in no way the ones who will decide whether they can stay in Germany or not.

4 Conclusion

The results described above show that by combining two different sets of research questions, each may enrich the other. On the one hand, focusing on the perspectives of refugee children by following a childhood studies paradigm provides a picture of the research subjects not as mere victims of structural discrimination, but as agents who find different ways to deal with the limitations to the possibilities of shaping their own lives.

On the other hand, it is the capabilities approach that makes it possible to talk of limitations. Through its operationalisation of a decent life, it also delivers an understanding of which aspects constrain a decent life and thereby goes beyond the mere description of children's perspectives. In this understanding, it is striking how comprehensively refugee children are excluded from material and symbolic resources and thus how the possibilities to develop their full human potential are being limited severely.

Hence, from a capabilities perspective that argues for equal rights, Leotrim's living situation can be described as materially deprived in comparison to local standards, even though Leotrim himself reports being satisfied with it. Nevertheless, that does not mean to devalue Leotrim's satisfaction, because it can be understood as an active engagement in the structures in which he is embedded.

By combining the capabilities approach and childhood studies in this way, the results of the study contribute to closing the research gap in the study of margizens and particularly of refugee children.

References

Anderson, Benedict R. O'G. (1985): Imagined Communities. Reflections on the Origin and Spread of Nationalism. London: Verso.

Chatty, Dawn/Crivello, Gina/Lewando Hundt, Gillian (2005): Theoretical and Methodological Challenges of Studying Refugee Children in the Middle East and North Africa: Young Palestinian, Afghan and Sahrawi Refugees. In: Journal of Refugee Studies, 18, 4, pp. 387–409.

Clark, Zoë/Eisenhuth, Franziska (2011): A Capabilities Perspective on Childhood and Youth. In: Leßmann, Ortrud/Otto, Hans-Uwe/Ziegler, Holger (eds.): Closing the Capabilities Gap. Renegotiating Social Justice for the Young. Opladen: Barbara Budrich, pp. 277–285.

Feagin, Joe R./McKinney, Karyn (2003): The Many Costs of Racism. Oxford: Rowman.

Fraser, Nancy (2008): Scales of Justice. Reimagining Political Space in a Globalizing World. Cambridge: Polity Press.

Glaser, Barney G./Strauss, Anselm L. (1979): The Discovery of Grounded Theory. Strategies for Qualitative Research. 10th print. New York: Aldine.

James, Allison (2009): Agency. In: Qvortrup, Jens/Corsaro, William A./Honig, Michael-Sebastian (eds.): The Palgrave Handbook of Childhood Studies. London: Palgrave, pp. 34–45.

James, Allison/Prout, Alan (2007): A New Paradigm for the Sociology of Childhood? Provenance, Promise and Problems. In: James, Allison/Prout, Alan (eds.): Constructing and Reconstructing Childhood: Contemporary Issues in the Sociological Study of Childhood. 2nd edition. London: Routledge Falmer, pp. 7–33.

James, Allison/Prout, Alan (1995): Hierarchy, Boundary and Agency: Toward a Theoretical Perspective on Childhood. In: Mandell, Nancy (ed.): Sociological Studies of Children. Volume 7. Middlesex: Jai Press Inc., pp. 77–99.

Martiniello, Marco (1994): Citizenship of the European Union. A Critical View. In: Bauböck, Rainer (ed.): From Aliens to Citizens. Redefining the Status of Immigrants in Europe. Aldershot: Avebury, pp. 29–47.

Menon, Nivedita (2002): Universalism without foundations? Book reviewed. Martha C. Nussbaum (2000) Women and Human Development: The Capabilities Approach. Cambridge: Cambridge University Press. In: Economy and Society, 31, 1, pp. 152–169.

Mohr, Katrin (2005): Stratifizierte Rechte und soziale Exklusion von Migranten im Wohlfahrtsstaat (Stratified Rights and Social Exclusion of Migrants in the Welfare State). In: Zeitschrift für Soziologie, 34, 5, pp. 383–398.

Nussbaum, Martha (2007): Frontiers of Justice. Disability, Nationality, Species Membership. 1st paperback edition. Cambridge: Harvard University Press.

Nussbaum, Martha (2000): Women and Human Development. The Capabilities Approach. Cambridge: University Press.

Prout, Alan (2000): Childhood Bodies: Construction, Agency and Hybridity. In: Prout, Alan (ed.): The Body, Childhood and Society. Basingstoke: Macmillan, pp. 1–18.

Sen, Amartya (1999): Development as Freedom. New York: Knopf.

Strauss, Anselm L./Corbin, Juliet (2008): Basics of Qualitative Research. Techniques and Procedures for Developing Grounded Theory. 3rd edition. Thousand Oaks: Sage.

Online sources

AsylbLG (Asylbewerberleistungsgesetz): Asylum Seekers' Benefit Act. http://www.gesetze-im-internet.de/bundesrecht/asylblg/gesamt.pdf [accessed 18/07/13] (There is no English online-version provided).

AsylVfG (Asylverfahrensgesetz): Asylum Procedure Act. http://www.gesetze-im-internet.de/englisch_asylvfg/asylum_procedure_act_(asylvfg).pdf [accessed 18/07/13].

AufenthG (Gesetz über den Aufenthalt, die Erwerbstätigkeit und die Integration von Ausländern im Bundesgebiet): Act on the Residence, Economic Activity and Integration of Foreigners in the Federal Territory. http://www.gesetze-im-internet.de/englisch_aufenthg/residence_act.pdf [accessed 18/07/13]

UN General Assembly (1989): Convention on the Rights of the Child. Adopted and opened for signature, ratification and accession by General Assembly resolution 44/25 of 20 November 1989. http://www.ohchr.org/Documents/ProfessionalInterest/crc.pdf [accessed 18/07/13].

UNHCR (n. d.): Children. http://www.unhcr.org/pages/49c3646c1e8.html [accessed 18/07/13].

Bettina Ritter

Capabilities of Young Mothers in Welfare Institutions: What Can the Capability Approach Learn From Biographical Research?

1 Young motherhood and a capabilities perspective

In Germany, women under the age of 20 give birth to about one per cent of all babies a year (see Spies 2008). Although the numbers of "teenage mothers" in Germany have been relatively stable for more than a decade now, it is nevertheless a popular topic in the media. It began to be discussed more frequently and broadly at the beginning of the 2000s, when, related to a change in the system of statistical returns, the belief became widespread that the actual number of teenage pregnancies had risen. Nowadays, it is only an infrequent topic in broadsheet newspapers and political debates, but a frequent subject of several documentaries and docusoaps on television.

In its structure, the way it is discussed in the public and represented in these television series is quite similar to the debate in countries with higher rates such as the United States or Great Britain (see UNICEF 2001). Besides the overall opinion that young motherhood is a social problem and somehow bad for either the young mother, the baby, or society (see Auletta 1999, Murray 1996), it is also seen as the result and, at the same time, as the cause of problematic development in the young mother. Whereas some researchers and scientists follow this perspective, there has been a strong reaction against this argumentation among several researchers, especially in Great Britain, who have delivered the evidence for an "alternative view" (Geronimus 1991) on young motherhood that fits a capabilities perspective. Their main results can be summarized by the four following major findings:

First, young pregnancy and motherhood could and can be a rather unproblematic event for young women. Considering that pregnancy and parenthood may well not be an easy development for women and their families no matter their age, it has been shown that outcomes are shaped most powerfully by poverty, and not by the timing of motherhood in the life course (Ermisch/Pevalin 2003).

Second, young pregnancy and motherhood sometimes even have a positive influence on the life situation of young women and constitute a moment of emancipation from diverse constraints (Cater/Coleman 2006). As, for example, Phoenix (1991) already showed in her study, pregnancy could be a turning point for young women in terms of planning for the future: forming a strong family unit, making renewed efforts to gain qualifications, or turning away from drug usage for instance.

Third, with motherhood as a symbol of adult status (Schofield 1994) and the socially idealized form of womanhood (Phoenix et al. 1991), many young mothers build a positive identity as being a good mother. For them, it is a source of self-worth and social legitimation. Nevertheless, research has also shown that this construction of a mother identity is aggravated for young women because they are positioned (by virtue of their age and often class) outside the dominant cultural norms of motherhood (McDermott/Graham 2005).

Fourth, young motherhood could be a meaningful option for some young women. Most qualitative research has shown that these young women are reflexively creating their own self-identities and life narratives. But from a capabilities perspective, we have to consider that for most young mothers, "the choices available for their biographies are limited both by structural inequalities and by the absence of positive discourse" (McDermott/Graham 2005: 72). In this sense, they are aware of their own life options and "possible selves" (Markus/Nurius 1986) and form their orientations accordingly (Grundmann 2008). Most young mothers have a realistic appraisal of the opportunities and possibilities present in the immediate environment as well as one's own personal capabilities (e.g. Arai 2009a). The decision to become a mother could then represent a meaningful life option and can be seen as a normative and reasonable option for some young women (e.g. Dash 1989, Phoenix 1991, Jewell et al. 2000, SmithBattle 2000). In some families or communities, early fertility may even be commonplace and in this way normative. That does of course affect how it is experienced. "Early motherhood often made sense in terms of local constitutions of opportunity, constraint, and social practice." (Duncan et al. 2010: 18).

Similar to the findings of McDermott and Graham (2005) who compiled a wide review of studies from Great Britain, the most problematic conditions for young mothers in my study turned out to be not only the experience of stigma but also poverty and multiple social disadvantages. I shall not elaborate in depth on the aspect of stigma in this chapter. But the assumptions about "normal" and "right" motherhood underlying stigmatization processes play an important role, because this is not only a matter of personal interactions but also evident in policy and societal institutions such as work, family, and the social services.

In the next section, I shall discuss the topic of young motherhood in relation to the concept of the normal life course and the welfare state as a life-course regime. In the following section, I shall present two perspectives –

biography and capabilities – as a way to overcome a normal life-course perspective, especially in research. I shall show that the CA and biographical research share some main principles that are useful when investigating young mothers' lives and their experiences with welfare institutions. I shall refer to some results of a biographical study on young mothers by presenting the examples of two cases and then close the chapter with conclusions for future research and policymaking.

2   Young mothers and the "normal life course"

This chapter refers to a biographical case study on young women who gave birth before the age of 20 and who either lived in a social services institution or were engaged in vocational training in one. The study was conducted from 2010 to 2012 in a large city in Germany. In total, 17 autobiographical-narrative interviews were carried out. Three of the interviewees were selected according to the principle of theoretical sampling as contrasting cases and were analysed in depth with structural narration analysis. This method of biography analysis was developed by Fritz Schütze (e.g. 1987) on the empirical basis of autobiographical narratives. Two of these analyses will be presented in this chapter. Because all interviewees were clients of welfare institutions and services, the context of the German welfare state and its social policy has to be reflected and taken into account:

According to the typology of Esping-Andersen (1990), Germany is a conservative "life-course regime" that "promotes a continuous life course" (Leisering 2004: 216). Because the life course is structured by age (and age norms), social policy targets defined age groups. "Socially defined age – rather than need – becomes a criterion for benefits and services" (Leisering 2004: 214). The welfare state and life-course policy are, according to Kohli (1987), linked within the "working society". The role of social policy is then to provide security and control in the spheres outside of work (wage labour) – so-called decommodification (Esping-Anderson 1990) – and insofar to support a "transformation of non-wage labourers into wage labourers" (Offe 1984: 94). The central role of work in the organization of society becomes obvious when looking at social insurance and social benefits in general. "Major benefits depend on individual contributions made during working life, with normal being positively rewarded by social insurance. More than in many other welfare states, this is done in a gendered way – differences between male and female life courses are reinforced by social policy" (Leisering 2004: 218). In line with this discriminating effect on women, Levy (1977: 43) distinguishes between a male and a female "normal biography", with the female biography not complying with the "tripartite model of the life course in the 'work society' – preparing for work (education), working, retiring ..." (Leisering 2004: 212). This structure comes together with a strong notion of the traditional nuclear family that is also reflected in German family policy and law. Nevertheless, contemporary social policy strategies target women in a double sense: on the one hand, the main responsibility for childcare is still allocated to them; whereas, on the other hand, gender equality is fully implemented by law. This two-pronged policy leads to a special disadvantage for working class mothers: Obliged to compete with everyone else on the labour market, they are more likely to have difficulties in reconciling motherhood and work. They not only have to compete for more insecure and poorly paid jobs – if they find one at all – but they also suffer more from a lack of material resources to organize childcare.

Concerning young mothers, the preparation for (education) and/or inclusion into the labour market is the imperative in social policy strategies, social work practice, and public debate. According to the "social integrationist discourse" (Levitas 1998), the inclusion of "the excluded" into society via inclusion into labour work is supposed to be the key to individual well-being as well as the cohesion of society. When it comes to young motherhood, that discourse is linked to the "moral underclass discourse" (Levitas 1998) which states that young mothers are characterized mainly by a lack of morals. The "alternative view", presented above, fits with neither these discourses nor current policy that aims primarily to prevent young pregnancy and considers it to be a social problem per se (e.g. SEU 1999). On a policy level, this alternative view is rarely discussed (see Arai 2009b). Instead, a perspective that focuses on individual failure blinds out issues and problems of social structure.

From the perspective of the Capability Approach (CA), the aim would be to promote opportunities for all young people and special support for young mothers in order to promote their well-being. A perspective that aims to prevent young pregnancy per se does not match a capabilities perspective that attempts to enhance people's freedoms of choice. Furthermore, the discussion on young motherhood refers mostly to the "normal life course" from which these young women deviate as belonging to neither "normal" youth nor "normal" adulthood (or motherhood). The social construction of a "normal life course" and its societal regulation has a strong impact on (young) people in general and on young mothers in particular. This is most likely to stand counter to the opportunity freedom of people, because it restricts opportunities to participate in what is characteristic for each phase of the "normal life course". Individual interests and ideas about how to conduct one's own life are no longer supported as soon as they contradict those societal constructions of normality and the political regulation of the "work society" – and this is (mostly) the case with young motherhood.

My assumption is that a capabilities perspective can overcome a linear life-course perspective that, especially in the case of young mothers, does not help to investigate and improve their real agency freedom and capabilities. By focusing on opportunities and agency, it is possible to respect the individual person beyond the normal life course and work. This calls for a research approach that focuses on the individual biography and individual experiences, and investigates social processes and structures through a subjective account. A biographical-narrative method is one approach to realize this in research.

3 Biographical Research and a Capabilities Perspective

Nowadays, the research methodology of biographical-narrative interviewing is well established within qualitative research in the social sciences. It aims to explore social reality through the reconstruction of biographies by analysing the real-life stories of people. This follows the principles of reconstructive analysis.

The basic reason for the enactment of the autobiographical narrative interview is the assumption that social reality is not just experienced and bestowed with meaning by individual actors with their unique life histories, but in addition that it is produced, is supported and kept in force, is endured with pain and suffered, is protested at and turned over or even destroyed as well as it is gradually changed by individual actors with their personal life histories and involved biographical identity developments. […] Thus, taking individual life histories and analysing them is a promising avenue to social reality. (Schütze 2007: 2)

Biography as a "mirror" to socialized subjectivity delivers insights into the social structuring of individual, biographical sense-making and shows how individual (re)constructions of one's own life story are at the same time expressions of the socially general (see Hanses 2010: 117). It is never just one societal structure, essentially true story of individual experience, practice of discourse, or subjective self-concept; it is always all of it – in a dialectical and contradictory way (see Hanses 2010: 114). Hence, because biography is not only an individual or psychological category but also a social construct that generates patterns of individual processing of experiences in social context, it always reflects social conditions and discourses (see Völter et al. 2009: 7). These can be reconstructed through biographical analysis methods. However, the interweaving of structure and individual can be analysed not only in every single case but also by comparing different cases. With the method of theoretical sampling (see Glaser/Strauss 1967), the research process moves, in the manner of theoretical saturation (Strauss 1987), towards a comparison or even a typology of generalizable biographical patterns (Krüger 2006).

"Assuming that biographic narrative expression is expressive both of conscious concerns and also of unconscious cultural, societal and individual presuppositions and processes" (Wengraf 2011: 50), I consider the special strength of biographical research in the light of the Capabilities Approach to consist especially in the two shared principles: the principle of freedom as a process and the principle of general openness.

3.1 Freedom as a process

By analysing biographies, it is possible to take the individual into account with her "positional" and "situated agency" (see Zimmermann 2006). This can then correspond with an understanding of freedom that "engages agency and environment in a dynamic and interactive way" (Zimmermann 2006: 478). In this way, the conception of freedom becomes oriented more towards the possibilities of action instead of being tendentially essentialist and substantive as Sen (1999) conceptualizes it. Instead of considering freedom as a state that people have or do not have in a given situation, a biographical approach discusses "freedom as a process" in its temporal dynamic during the life course (Zimmermann 2006): freedom as a process of liberation, as interactive relation, as process of power relations and interaction. This implies a "historical" account to explain the movement towards the present (Wengraf 2011: 54). The biographical approach emphasizes the processuality and temporality of social phenomena, of individual situations, and of social structure. The dimension of becoming – also with a perspective towards the future – implies a notion of time and change.[1]

3.2 The principle of openness

The research process as such is characterized by a special openness to subjective sense-making and the patterns of experiences of the interviewees. Pre-existing theoretical knowledge in the researcher is necessary to gain access to the subject, but it has to be reflected on and documented transparently (Strübing 2004). The concept of sensitivity (Strauss 1987) points to the importance of not overwhelming the research subject with one's own pre-existing theoretical or personal concepts. Therefore, the whole research process can be described as theory-developing rather than theory-proving. In the

---

1   The construct of biography itself is also subject to historicity, because as a medium of self-portrait and self-expression, it is linked to the emergence of modern society (see Alheit 1990, Bourdieu 1998).

analysis, the researcher does not subsume under predefined categories, but develops relevant categories out of the data. Especially with the topic of young motherhood, which is mostly researched on and discussed with various, mostly condemning presuppositions, this methodology seems to be an adequate approach to the reality of these young women. Foreknowledge and judgements on the research objective have to be reflected on because these constitute the glasses through which the researcher is looking at her research objective and the interview data. The principle of openness is also given in the interview technique and the interview structure: At the beginning of the interview, the researcher should give only one open question that gives the so-called stimulus for the interviewee to begin her narration of the live story. Schütze calls this extempore autobiographical story-telling because it is not a prepared story, but a spontaneously evolving narration.

In contrast to semi-structured, strongly guiding qualitative methods or even quantitative standardized methods, this "allows or requires the interviewee to give their own form and sequence to what they choose to recall and tell" (Wengraf 2011: 52). In the second part of the interview, the interviewer asks concrete questions according to what has been told before. Hence, the decision about what is relevant lies in the hands of the interviewee, and there is no pre-justification of relevance by the interviewer through giving fixed interview guidelines or questionnaires.[2]

One consequence of the principle of openness is that with the construct of biography, the researcher does not have to focus on a specific topic or live domain but gains a holistic insight into the individual instead. In this way, interconnected life domains do not have to be split up artificially (see Becker-Schmidt 1987). The decision on which areas of life will be the main focus remains with the interviewee and is not made by the researcher in advance.

There are two ways in which this principle is beneficial for a capabilities oriented research perspective. First, it allows a holistic assessment of the capabilities of an individual by taking the whole person and her life with both past and future aspects into account. It also takes the idea of ethical individualism seriously by giving voice to the single person. Moreover, the strong need for reflexivity of the researcher within the research process of biographical-narrative research can prevent one possible pitfall of the CA: the measurement of capabilities in terms of an idea of success in life. Depending on what sphere researchers focus on, it is the accomplishment of a specific task or step into an actual state of being (functioning) they assess. CA research on youth and education, for example, often has the implicit idea of success as finishing school and then finally "accomplishing the entrance into the occu-

---

2   Nevertheless, it is easily possible to supplement this method with a more structured and guidelined interview at the end. But both may be combined only after being analysed separately from each other.

pational system" (Grundmann/Dravenau 2010). This pitfall is not part of the CA itself, but can become one quite easily when researchers lack awareness or when they are doing commissioned research. A similar potential problem emerges within biographical research. Therefore it is absolutely necessary to meet the requirements of reflexivity as a researcher, be aware of one's own ideas of normativity, of right life practice and a "normal" life course, and to not bring these assumptions into the research process as an evaluative frame.

Especially in biographical research on women, this has been criticized as an unjustified measurement that has too often been accompanied by a white male bias (Dausien 1994). Instead of the assumption of a linear life model according to the societal beliefs of a normal (male) life course with a working career in the centre, it can be a special strength of biographical research to reconstruct disruptions, changes, and turning points as well. This would be in the spirit of the CA, because it makes (female) disadvantages and limited options visible.

3.3 Normality beliefs as a possible pitfall for research analysis

If researchers do not apply the imperative of reflexion during the research process consistently, they run the risk of getting trapped in the pitfall of unquestioned judgement: implicit valuation of success and failure according to their own measures of normality and the dominant idea of a normal life course. The combination of both approaches, the CA and biographical research, can guide researchers to not make this mistake in the analysis process: (a) the strong notion of own reasonable values of the persons (other than the researcher herself) can protect researchers from that pitfall. (b) This emphasizes the research perspective of qualitative, reconstructive research in general and biographical-narrative research in particular, because principles are developed out of the data and not set beforehand and then applied to the data.

The need for this awareness is especially obvious with the topic of young motherhood. As feminist researchers have been pointing out, researchers have often used a male and middle-class ideal as a golden standard. Categories such as success, linearity, progress, education, and career have been used to evaluate biographies and life courses (see Dausien 1994: 136). But, in contrast, an image of the "female normal biography" (see Levy 1977) can also lead to condemnation and moral evaluation. This makes it necessary to be sensitive to turning points, changes, and disruptions, because these often characterize female biographies in comparison to assumed "normal" male biographies.[3]

---

3   Most men also reveal a discrepancy between the institutionalized norm of the life course and their experienced biography. Nonetheless, this study focuses on young women because they reveal these phenomena exceedingly strongly.

4 Capabilities of young mothers

When working with a capabilities perspective in research, one has (usually) two main questions in mind: First, to ask about the freedom of people to choose what they value with good reasons, and second, what in terms of structure *and* the individual enables this scope of freedom or diminishes it, and in what ways. This section presents some research results showing how this perspective could be realized through a biographical research approach towards the phenomena of young motherhood.

The main issues that have emerged through reconstructive analysis are the following:

- Becoming of the persons. Relevant factors such as the family constellation, material situation, local space, persons, and so forth that have influenced the becoming
- Sense-making processes in relation to young motherhood then taking a procedural perspective
- Development of own values, life plans, and biographical strategies
- Experiences of deprivation and agency
- Processing of socio-cultural norms on youth, motherhood, and work
- Mechanisms of enablement (conversion factors): opportunity freedom

All of the young mothers who participated in the study are situated in a struggle between youth, labour work, and motherhood. They are affected differently and meet the tension between these (conflicting) poles in different ways ranging from conformity to resistance. How far they are able to develop resistant mothering practices, have a stable employment perspective, and have access to youth-related space for identity development can be ascribed largely to the (biographical) resources they can draw on. It also depends on how far their own life plan and way of living meet societal expectations. The study discloses how far societal requirements counteract the setting of relevance of the young mothers themselves. In the following, I shall illustrate this in two selected cases. First, I shall give a short biographical portrait of each case before analysing them in terms of both the degree of freedom and the constraints that shape these young mothers' possibilities to build their own life plans and to actually realise them.

4.1 Two biographies – two different experiences of young motherhood

Case 1: Annika was 16, when she got pregnant. At the time of the interview, she is 17 years old and living with her 1-year-old daughter in an institutional home. After her child was born, she started to go back to the school she quit when she became pregnant. Her orientation towards family is strongly developed, whereas her orientation towards wage labour is weak. The importance of family is present in the whole life story: she cares a lot about her parents and siblings and has a very close relationship to them. She worries about her father and has a strong empathy with her family members and their situation. She defends them and keeps the family together. Against this backdrop, she focuses on building her own family. Her plan to have a child is embedded in a love story with her (former) boyfriend and in the dream of having an idyllic "traditional nuclear family" life (see Kortendiek 2010). But the sphere of family is, of course, not free from conflicts and contradiction (see Becker-Schmidt 2008), and her expectations have not been met. Her boyfriend struggles with his life and cannot manage to fulfil the role of the father and husband in the manner that she wishes. So she ends up bearing sole responsibility for their child and having to live in an institutional home for young mothers. Because it is expected from her by the social workers and professionals in the social services, and because there are no economic resources available to her (e.g. through the father of the child or her parents), she is forced to develop an occupational life plan after all.

Even though Annika's orientation is initially more of an either–or between a focus on labour market and family, the dominant norm for a "normal" women's life course nowadays expects the integration of family and work. This leads to a female life model that includes part-time occupation, household, and care work at the same time. This is also what is expected from young mothers – and especially explicitly from those who live in institutional homes and are therefore under special surveillance and guidance (Wallner 2010).

In Annika's case, the institutions of social services urge her to pursue a plan of doing vocational training. In her counselling sessions, it is suggested that she should attempt training as a childcare worker, which has a clear gender and class bias because it is a rather low-skilled, insecure, and poorly paid job. Content-wise, that might fit her preferences perfectly, but in her life story it becomes clear that it was in no way a decision that she had made, but one that was made for her. Any degree of argumentation or evaluation of that plan is missing in the story she tells. She does not have any motivation or reasoning concerning this plan, but knows that she has to follow it. In her case, because the control aspect of the institution is so prominent, she also fears losing her child if she fails to meet the diverse requirements imposed on her. This concerns not only the pressure to get engaged in the labour market, but also her behaviour and life style in general.

In terms of freedom, Annika's case is multi-layered. She is trapped in multiple dependencies and a structure of requirements. There is, as just explained, the compulsion for "double socialization" (see Becker-Schmidt 2008) but with the responsibility to be shouldered only by her. This is why, to some extent, she has had to adapt her original life plan of prioritizing motherhood and starting a family rather than developing her own working career to these deprived circumstances. However, this has not been accepted, and she was unable to convert her ideas into reality. Her new life plan is heavily compelled, but she tries her best to meet all requirements. From that perspective, Annika possesses the biographical agency to deal with her situation. But there is almost no space available for her to take a stand against the external requirements and act intractably. Family as a synonym for love, care, and happiness (Kortendiek 2010: 443) is supposed to provide what is presumably not possible to find anywhere else: solidarity, love, care, and closeness (Böhnisch 2005: 225). Annika distances herself from the heavy risks the labour market would most likely expose her to. But because she is compelled to be the only person responsible for the well-being of her child, both spheres (wage labour and childcare) are quite problematic for her to handle. The institutions of the social services provide some practical support, but function primarily as the entity that arrogates the demands of the welfare state and its society – with all the accompanying ramifications.

Case 2: Heide was 19 years old when she got pregnant. At the time of the interview, her son is already 7 years old. In contrast to Annika, Heide's life story is all about the special value of individual fulfilment and freedom. She proudly separates herself and her life from any normality right from the very start by being capable of speaking another language, having a different everyday life, and a different family arrangement in her childhood than anyone else. But throughout the life story, it becomes obvious that she cannot fight against the enforcements of society. She quit school after 10th grade and worked in temporary jobs in order to make just enough money to get by and to travel. Even though her chances for a working career were quite good, because she still had a high school diploma despite quitting grammar school, she did not want to enter vocational training and especially not the one she is doing at the time of the interview. But she had to do this because she could not find an adequate job without a completed vocational training. Heide feels heavily trapped in her uniform everyday life but – and that is the only point when her motherhood becomes an obstacle for her – she cannot break out until her son finishes primary school. She prefers freedom and spontaneity over security and safety and plans for a life that secures a minimum existence for herself (and her son) to but allows her to be more independent. In that future, imagination work (e.g. shearing sheep in New Zealand) would be more than just securing her economic situation. It would provide her with self-fulfilment. She has the idea of fleeing to somewhere far away in hopes of finding more freedom there, because she cannot imagine that she will find it by making only slight changes to her current situation. Remarkably, she is able to imagine an idealistic life notably beyond her normality and the logic of her current situation. This constitutes a strong contrast between the feeling of constraints in her current life situation (mainly in terms of time and work) and a feeling of freedom in her future imagination.

4.2 Addressing young mothers and the consequences for their capabilities

Young mothers are mostly addressed in relation to their motherhood and to their working career (Wallner 2010). The women in this study are clients of the youth welfare service, other social services, and the Public Employment Agency. Those institutions with which they (have to) deal regularly in their everyday life transmit – directly or indirectly – the societal expectations regarding young women. The young mothers in this study experience that professionals in the institutional homes are more concerned about the "right" conduct of life and "right" motherhood practice; and in training institutions, the imperative of labour work is dominant. The study found that this one-sided addressing of the women – who are already deprived and vulnerable – leads to even more capability deprivation in young mothers.

The support Annika (Case 1) gets from the institutional home concentrates on the two features of the normal adult female life course: motherhood and wage work. Institutions of the youth welfare service that offer stationary accommodation for young women who give birth under the age of 26 are regulated by law.[4] This law reflects the orientation of the institutions: the main focus is supposed to be the establishment of the caring/mothering ability[5] in the women and the accomplishment of their own education. This approach lacks any orientation towards the person's freedom, values, or opportunities in general. Support with childcare is given to enable the young mother to go to school. Therefore, the social workers, for example, bring the child to school so she can breastfeed her there during breaks. Childcare at other times of the day and for other purposes is not provided. Annika, for example, is allowed to attend a pottery course for 2 hours once a week. This was suggested to her because she is supposed to improve her patience and calmness in order to become a "better" mother. Other support focuses on aspects of the organization of everyday life. How to behave is regulated strongly, especially via time rules: when to do what (e.g. cleaning the kitchen) when to come

4 §19 SGB VIII
5 In German *Erziehungsfähigkeit*.

home, where to go, with whom, or for how long. These regulations also include the handling of the child, for example, who is allowed to take care of her, when, and for how long. Annika is, for example, not allowed to stay away overnight and leave the child at her parents' home, even though they offer to take care of her. That would be a concrete resource that could provide access to the youth-related freedom that she personally values, but this does not fit the focus of the institution.

Moreover, young mothers in vocational training have to handle being addressed in a one-sided way by the social services. The (part-time) training especially for young mothers has been established by the social services and is promoted by the public employment agency. Heide, for example, is doing a vocational training in boatbuilding. Because this measure targets only the young mother's perspectives on the labour market, she is dependent on further support from her family. In Heide's case, this has mainly been money and emotional support when she was still living with her mother. Now that her mother is living in another country, this is support with childcare during especially time-consuming phases of her training (exams, immersion courses in school). Whereas the first focuses on her as a person, childcare focuses on her working career through completion of training.

For both cases, the fact that they cannot share the general mothering responsibility but are exclusively responsible is the main problem they both have to deal with. This is a fact that the institutions do not question but set as an actuality that has to be handled by the young mothers as one task of "good" mothering. leads In this society, the ideal of "double socialization" imposes a "double burden" on women (Böllert 2010). The welfare institutions consider this as "normality" for young mothers well. This reproduces gender inequality in terms of an acquired one-sided responsibility for the child.

5 Conclusion

As the examples in the empirical analysis show, young mothers have to deal with a discrepancy between, on the one side, societal expectations and the organization of work and family and, on the other side, their own imaginings of life. The discussions above raise the question whether the institutions of the social services (especially the institutional homes) are more of an additional burden rather than a factor that could actually relieve the young women from some of their societal strains. This points to what Lessenich calls the two standards of the welfare state: the coercive and the enabling dimensions of its actions (Lessenich 2012: 10). For young mothers, the enabling dimension is the everyday support they receive from the welfare institutions in terms of childcare, material support, and accommodation. The coercive dimension lies in the age-wise structuring of the life course centred on work – a normality they can barely match. The results of the study suggest the ways in which the welfare institutions put a one-sided effort into fitting young mothers into the functionings related to the "normal life course" with a focus on integration into the labour market. This is not helpful in terms of the CA. To broaden their opportunity freedom and their capability set, the focus would have to be on enabling the young women to have youth-characteristic freedom with no prescribed outcome instead and on opening up real opportunities for them to shape their own life (plans). Support has to be flexible to meet every person's life plans and interests and offer part-time occupations, part-time education, longer opening hours for childcare facilities, living facilities with diverse housing structures, and social work provisions that address young mothers simply as young people. The precondition of financial stability has to be secured by the welfare state without binding these benefits to one's position in relation to the labour market, but in relation to one's needs.

In this sense, the CA could be not only a political instrument (as it functions in, for example, the United Nations Development Program) but also a research perspective – as outlined above. Research could analyse the actual system by investigating the experiences and suffering of people, by asking how processes of exploitation work, and why the system functions as it does. A biographical approach is appropriate for this analysis, because it is linked directly to the experiences and practices of people and allows a holistic perspective. Accordingly, for the topic of young motherhood, a CA perspective combined with a biographical approach views the individual life story as the anchor for social practices. It does not assess a normal life course and possible deviances, but can explore how people deal with possible discrepancies between their biography and the societally supported normal life course. It can investigate how people make sense of societal guidelines, how they perceive institutions of the welfare state in terms of enablement or restriction, and how they master their lives, even though not fitting into the age-structured frame of social policy with all its consequences.

The main principle that both approaches – the CA and a biographical perspective – have in common is to view subjectivity as being situated in terms of time and space and as being socialized. Hence, both are interested in the linkage between structural and individual aspects: bringing together the personal ability to do something and the social structures that either do or do not promote this. The focus lies on the consequences that evolve for the individual's opportunities for acting and shaping one's own life. Individual agency in social context and structures is the main focus of the CA and it is already included in the methodology of biographical research as a general perspective. Vice versa, a biographical research paradigm strengthens the CA's focus on the socialized individual and her practices and experiences. Therefore, the concrete research interest in the capabilities of individuals can be met by using this as a focus for analysing the empirical data.

References

Alheit, Peter (1990): Alltag und Biographie. Studien zur gesellschaftlichen Konstitution biographischer Perspektiven. Bremen: Univ.-Buchh.
Arai, Lisa (2009a): Teenage Pregnancy. The making and unmaking of a problem. Bristol: Policy Press.
Arai, Lisa (2009b): What a difference a decade makes: rethinking teenage pregnancy as a problem. In: Social Policy & Society, 8, 2, pp. 171–183.
Auletta, Ken (1999): The Underclass. Woodstock, New York: The Overlook Press.
Becker-Schmidt, Regina (1987): Die doppelte Vergesellschaftung – die doppelte Unterdrückung: Besonderheiten der Frauenforschung in den Sozialwissenschaften. In: Unterkircher, Lilo/Wagner, Ina (eds.): Die andere Hälfte der Gesellschaft. Österreichischer Soziologentag 1985. Soziologische Befunde zu geschlechtsspezifischen Formen der Lebensbewältigung. Wien: Verlag des Österreichischen Gewerkschaftsbundes, pp. 10–25.
Becker-Schmidt, Regina (2008): Doppelte Vergesellschaftung von Frauen: Divergenzen und Brückenschläge zwischen Privat- und Erwerbsleben. In: Becker, Ruth/Kortendiek, Barbara (eds.): Handbuch Frauen- und Geschlechterforschung. Theorie, Methoden, Empirie. Wiesbaden: VS Verlag, pp. 65–74.
Böhnisch, Lothar (2005): Sozialpädagogik der Lebensalter. Eine Einführung. 4th revised ed. Weinheim/München: Juventa.
Böllert, Karin (2010): Frauen in Familienverhältnissen: Zur Vereinbarkeit von Familie und Beruf. In: Böllert, Karin/Oelkers, Nina (eds.): Frauenpolitik in Familienhand? Neue Verhältnisse in Konkurrenz, Autonomie oder Kooperation. Wiesbaden: VS Verlag, pp. 99–110.
Bourdieu, Pierre (1998): Die biographische Illusion. In: Bourdieu, Pierre: Praktische Vernunft. Zur Theorie des Handelns. Frankfurt/M.: Suhrkamp, pp. 75–82.
Cater, Suzanne/Coleman, Cater (2006): "Planned" teenage pregnancy. Perspectives of young parents from disadvantaged backgrounds. Bristol: The Policy Press.
Dash, Leon (1989): When children want children: The urban crisis of teenage childbearing. Urbana-Champaign/Chicago/Springfield: University of Illinois Press.
Dausien, Bettina (1994): Biographieforschung als "Königinnenweg"?: Überlegungen zur Relevanz biographischer Ansätze in der Frauenforschung. In: Diezinger, Angelika/Kitzer, Hedwig/Anker, Ingrid/Bingel, Irma/Haas, Erika/Odierna, Simone (eds.): Erfahrung mit Methode. Wegesozialwissenschaftlicher Frauenforschung. Freiburg: Kore, pp. 129–153.
Duncan, Simon/Edwards, Rosalind/Claire, Alexander (2010): Teenage parenthood: What's the Problem? London: The Tufnell Press.

Ermisch, John/Pevalin, David J. (2003): Who has a child as a teenager? ISER working paper 2003–30. Colchester: Institute for Social and Economic Research, University of Essex.
Esping-Andersen, Gosta (1990): The Three Worlds of Welfare Capitalism. Cambridge: Polity Press.
Geronimus, Arline T. (1991): Teenage Childbearing and Personal Responsibility: An Alternative View. In: Political Science Quarterly, 112, 3, pp. 405–430.
Glaser, Barney G./Strauss, Anselm L. (1967): The Discovery of Grounded Theory. Strategies for Qualitative Research. Piscataway: Transaction Publishers.
Grundmann, Matthias (2008): Handlungsbefähigung – eine sozialisationstheoretische Perspektive. In: Otto, Hans-Uwe/Ziegler, Holger (eds.): Capabilities – Handlungsbefähigung und Verwirklichungschancen in der Erziehungswissenschaft. Wiesbaden: VS Verlag, pp. 131–142.
Grundmann, Michael/Dravenau, Daniel (2010): Class, Agency and Capability. In: Otto, Hans-Uwe/Ziegler, Holger (eds.): Education, Welfare and the Capability Approach. A European Perspective. Opladen, Farmington Hills: Barbara Budrich Publishers, pp. 85–102.
Hanses, Andreas (2010): Biografie. In: Bock, Karin/Miethe, Ingrid (eds.): Handbuch qualitative Methoden in der Sozialen Arbeit. Opladen: Verlag Barbara Budrich, pp. 113–123.
Jewell, David/Tacchi, Jo/Donovan, Jenny (2000): Teenage pregnancy: whose problem is it? In: Family Practice, 17, pp. 522–528.
Kohli, Martin (1987): Die Institutionalisierung des Lebenslaufs. Historische Befunde und theoretische Argumente. In: Kölner Zeitschrift für Soziologie und Sozialpsychologie, 37, pp. 1–29.
Kortendiek, Beate (2010): Familie. Mutterschaft und Vaterschaft zwischen Traditionalisierung und Modernisierung. In: Becker, Ruth/Kortendiek, Beate (eds.): Handbuch der Frauen und Geschlechterforschung. Theorie, Methoden, Empirie. Wiesbaden: VS Verlag, pp. 442–453.
Krüger, Heinz-Hermann (2006): Entwicklungslinien, Forschungsfelder und Perspektiven der erziehungswissenschaftlichen Biographieforschung. In: Krüger, Heinz-Hermann/Marotzki, Winfried (eds.): Handbuch erziehungswissenschaftliche Biographieforschung. Wiesbaden: VS Verlag, pp. 13–34.
Leisering, Lutz (2004): Government and the Life Course. In: Mortimer, Jeylan T./Shanahan, Michael J. (eds.): Handbook of the Life Course. New York: Springer, pp. 205–225.
Lessenich, Stephan (2012): Theorien des Sozialstaats zur Einführung. Hamburg: Junius Verlag.
Levitas, Ruth (1998): The Inclusive Society? Social Exclusion and New Labour. New York: Palgrave MacMillan.
Levy, Rene (1977): Der Lebenslauf als Statusbiographie. Die weibliche Normalbiographie in makrosoziologischer Perspektive. Stuttgart: Ferdinand Enke Verlag.
Markus, Hazel/Nurius, Paula (1986): Possible Selves. In: American Psychologist, 41, 9, pp. 954–969.
McDermott, Elizabeth/Graham, Hilary (2005): Resilient Young Mothering: Social Inequalities, Late Modernity and the "Problem" of "Teenage" Motherhood. In: Journal of Youth Studies, 8, 1, pp. 59–79.

Murray, Charles (1996): The Emerging British Underclass. In: Charles Murray and the Underclass: The Developing Debate. The IEA Health and Welfare Unit in association with The Sunday Times. London: Civitas Institute for the Study of Civil Society, pp. 23–53.
Offe, Claus (1984): Contradictions of the Welfare State. London: Hutchinson.
Phoenix, Ann (1991): Young Mothers? Cambridge: Polity Press.
Phoenix, Ann/Woollett, Anne/Lloyd, Eva (1991): Motherhood. Meanings, practices and ideologies. London, Newbury Park, CA: Sage publications.
Schofield, Gillian (1994): The youngest mothers: The experience of pregnancy and motherhood among young women of school age. Michigan: Avebury Publishing.
Schütze, Fritz (1987): Das narrative Interview in Interaktionsfeldstudien I, Studienbrief der FernUniversität Hagen.
Schütze, Fritz (2007): Biography analysis on the empirical base of autobiographical narratives – how to analyse autobiographical narratives interviews. Part 1. In: Biographical counselling in rehabilitative vocational training. Magdeburg: Magdeburg University.
Sen, Amartya (1999): Development as freedom. Oxford: Oxford University Press.
Social Exclusion Unit (1999). Teenage Pregnancy: Report by the Social Exclusion Unit. London: Stationery Office.
SmithBattle, Lee (2000): Developing a Caregiving Tradition in Opposition to One's Past: lessons from a Longitudinal Study of Teenage Mothers. In: Public Health Nursing, 17, 2, pp. 85–93.
Spies, Anke (2008): Zwischen Kinderwunsch und Kinderschutz. Babysimulatoren in der pädagogischen Praxis. Wiesbaden: VS Verlag.
Strauss, Anselm (1987): Qualitative research for Social Scientists. Cambridge: Cambridge University Press.
Strübing, Jörg (2004): Grounded Theory. Zur sozialtheoretischen und epistemologischen Fundierung des Verfahrens der empirisch begründeten Theoriebildung. Wiesbaden: VS Verlag.
UNICEF (2001): A League Table of Teenage Births in Rich Nations. The United Nations Children's Fund, Innocenti Report Card, Issue No. 3, July 2001. Florence: UNICEF Innocenti Research Centre.
Völter, Bettina/Dausien, Bettina/Lutz, Helma/Rosenthal, Gabriele (eds.) (2009): Biographieforschung im Diskurs. Wiesbaden: VS Verlag.
Wallner, Claudia (2010): Junge Mütter in der Kinder- und Jugendhilfe: Sanktioniert, moralisiert, vergessen oder unterstützt? In: Spies, Anke (ed.): Frühe Mutterschaft. Die Bandbreite der Perspektiven und Aufgaben angesichts einer ungewöhnlichen Lebenssituation. Baltmannsweiler: Schneider Verlag Hohengehren, pp. 47–75.
Wengraf, Tom (2011): Interviewing for life-histories, lived situations and ongoing personal experiencing using the Biographic-Narrative Interpretive Method (BNIM): The BNIM Short Guide bound with The BNIM Detailed Manual Or is the latter becoming a monstrous encyclopedia? Version 11.03a.
Zimmermann, Bénédicte (2006): Pragmatism and the Capability Approach. Challenges in Social Theory and Empirical Research. In: European Journal of Social Theory, 9, 4, pp. 467–484.

Natalia Karmaeva

Reframing Teaching: A New Chance of Agency for Teaching Academics in Germany

1 Introduction

The driving forces behind the transformations of the structures of the academic labour market in Germany are new public management policies such as the implementation of market principles for the evaluation of academic work and funding distribution, changes in budgeting mechanisms, and cost-cutting (see e.g. Henkel 2000; Krücken et al. 2007; Musselin 2011). The transformations are taking place in line with the implementation of the Bologna Process. These developments are leading to changes in the conditions and content of academic work including the components of research, teaching, and administration (Kehm 2012). For teaching, it means a standardization of teaching, a growing workload, and a trend towards separating teaching from research (see e.g. Musselin 2007, 2011).

Recent research findings demonstrate that academics are in favour of greater involvement in research, because research performance is pivotal for advancing their academic careers (Cummings/Shin 2013: 1). Thus, teaching load is a constraint in academic career development (Bloch et al. 2011: 6). However, paying more attention to teaching in higher education policy and academic research is especially important for improving the quality of work and employment, especially for those teaching in positions below a professorship. As soon as teaching is acknowledged as one of the major working activities of junior academics, improving chances for the professional development of those who teach could contribute to better teaching and learning and increase the attractiveness of academic employment. For personnel policies on the level of universities, it is important to not just have more information on the structure of teaching personnel, their teaching load, their types of teaching, and their professional background. It is also pivotal to understand how the academics who teach see themselves within the broader context of the academic labour market, how they relate themselves to professional contexts outside academia, and how they frame teaching as an academic work component that is meaningful for their future professional development. This kind of information would enable a more appropriate allocation and monitoring of personnel along with responsible career development planning and counselling. In this way, the identification of framings of teaching and the elaboration of the criteria for development evaluation based on information about what kind of work academics see as meaningful to them may might support the promotion of the principle of social responsibility in university personnel policies. Therefore, I conducted a qualitative study in which I asked teaching academics how they perceive their situation. The theoretical framework of the study is the Capability Approach (CA).

This chapter starts by outlining the state of the art in research and introducing the current study in both its theoretical and empirical aspects. The subsequent presentation of the results focuses on the issue of the framing of teaching and its contextualization, and is based on the analysis of some examples from an interview. It shows how particular framings of teaching and the teaching–research relation are confronted with the existing professional discourses and available academic career structures, and how this affects development in an academic's space of agency. The conclusions and the discussion in the final part of the chapter aim to highlight further research paths and possibilities.

2   Capability approach as a promising framework for this analysis

The CA (see Sen 1999) was chosen as the theoretical framework because it promotes the idea of introducing novel practices and overcoming existing ones that do not support the realization of the common good (Alkire 2002: 140).

When "the very existence of a novel possibility for action demands a re-evaluation of the status quo" (Alkire 2002: 140), the role of actors as agents in recognizing and pursuing new action paths should not be underestimated. This is one of the reasons why the current chapter focuses on agency.

In the CA, agency freedom and agency achievement constitute what Sabina Alkire (2002: 129f.) calls "process freedom": agency achievement "refers to the person's success in the pursuit of the totality of her considered goals and objectives"; and agency freedom is "one's freedom to bring about the achievements one values and which one attempts to produce". Here it can be noted that the process aspect is stressed in the definitions of agency, whereas the "meaning" aspect is something rather taken for granted. In the current chapter, the specific interest is in how teaching academics conceptualize their work, particularly teaching; in other words, what are the meanings of teaching and how can their dynamics be characterized and evaluated?

The diversity of existing values and preferences limits operationalization of the CA in the dimension of opportunities (see Comim 2001). Nonetheless,

I shall attempt to operationalize the CA in the space of agency. This is a promising appeal, because the CA calls for incorporation of a broader social context into the evaluation (e.g. Shin 2011), whereas the dynamic character of social structures has not been taken into consideration sufficiently in previous research. The analysis of framings of teaching will make it possible to capture the dynamics of meanings of academic work. These dynamics of meanings are central in agency analysis following the principles of Giddens' structuration theory (1984) that stresses the interrelation between agency and structures.

The analytical account of identity negotiation (see Meisenbach 2008) will be applied in this analysis. The dynamics of meanings can be analysed in terms of how academics frame teaching and relate it to different contexts and academic labour market structures. It is about the interplay of different meanings of work and their reformulation: how do academics deal with the existing structures when framing their work in a meaningful way? According to Meisenbach (2008: 259), scholars are calling for more attention to the meanings and consequences of occupation, work, and professionalism, and they are doing this in relation to identity negotiation. Linked to this, the social dynamics of teaching reveals aspects of the meaning of work and the structural conditions of work (these are the "symbolic" and the "material" dimensions in the social interactionist terminology for the analysis of work; see Meisenbach 2008).

According to Emirbayer (1997: 288), the meaning or framing of work on an individual or collective level permits the categorization of phenomena. Meaning thus makes a categorical basis of action; it can assure its stability.

Sociological approaches such as identity negotiation analysis can be used to gather rich data on structures and social dynamics, whereas the CA makes it possible to draw normative conclusions on these while focusing on the individual. It allows the identification of structures pivotal for development. The self-reflection aspect implies that when there is a contradiction in the framing of work, agency is affected negatively, because such a contradiction limits an actor's abilities to choose: an actor cannot choose under the given conditions.

Traditionally, the Humboldtian idea of a close link between teaching and research has been characteristic of the German university (Teichler 2013: 61; Krücken 2003; Ash 2006). This discourse implies that "teaching is more creative and qualitatively more demanding, if the teachers are concurrently involved in research, and that research benefits if the scholars are involved in teaching" (Teichler 2013: 61). The material reality of academic work indicates that teaching and research assignments are not distributed in a similar way across different academic positions. The Humboldian principle tends to manifest more in the positions of professors who have both teaching and research assignments. Junior academics are involved in teaching in various ways. Additionally, they are considered to be in a qualification stage as researchers (*Wissenschaftler*), or, in other words, future professors (Teichler 2013: 62). Being a researcher in Germany means engaging in a professional activity that is overwhelming. The life of a researcher includes a long and demanding qualification stage in which it is almost impossible to separate working life from private life, because research as is perceived as an activity engaging the whole person (see Krais 2008).

Following Meisenbach's principles (2008), the framings of academic work are challenged by the content of academic work as well as its changing structural conditions. In changing/emerging professional fields, in contrast, actors may formulate new framings; or in the case of less prestigious types of work, their framings struggle to overcome the existing societal and professional discourses. That is, framing is a conceptualization of work by an individual that is formulated in the "negotiation" between existing discourses and the material reality of her work in order to arrive at meaningful conceptualization. Moreover, it is the categorization that provides a basis for taking action.

That is, agency is about reframing or arriving at new meanings plus the re contextualization of these meanings. These recontextualizations lead to the formation of new arenas for action and the introduction of novel practices, that is, development in the broader sense.

The CA also allows an additional important remark regarding the consequences of the situations of contention or contradiction that emerge in the interviews on decision making and thus agency. Contentions in action orientations may disrupt decision making and thus lead to incoherence and inconsistency, which, in turn, following the principle of practical reasoning, has to be eliminated (see Alkire 2002: 106).

The theoretical framework can be summed up as follows: "self-reflection" – or reframing of teaching – is the basic foundation that has to be enabled for further development. "Resources" as social structures that support these framings are another important component enabling agency.

3 The study sample and methods

In my study, I was interested in how teaching academics frame their working tasks. The fieldwork took place in 2012 and the beginning of 2013. The sample consisted of 16 teaching academics (8 female and 8 male) from junior faculty (*NachwuchswissenschaftlerInnen*). The interviews were conducted in German, and I have translated the quotes cited in this chapter myself. The method of the problem-centred interview was applied in order to focus on the conceptualizations of teaching in relation to important career decisions (Witzel 1985). Interviewees were from different universities in Germany: a midsized university with a strong international research reputation in some subjects, a big technical university that is highly internationally prominent in research, a prominent academic research institute, and a mid-sized university with traditions from the eastern part of Germany that aims to become more renowned internationally in some subjects.

The interview partners were in the career stage of doing (9 interviewees) or having completed their doctorates (7 interviewees). They were involved in teaching and other professional activities at a sociology department, an educational science department, or an interdisciplinary doctoral training school. In the case of the education department, teaching demand was high due to the presence of teacher training programmes at the university; the department of education and sociology at the technical university was teaching subjects as a service discipline to future teachers as well. The sample also contained some academics who were self-employed or employed part-time with a half-position in research institutes and who teach occasionally.

The interview participants were from the social sciences representing education science, sociology, social work, and history. Their teaching load varied from 2 to 13 academic hours per week. Their positions at the universities and in the research institute were diverse.

The doctoral students receiving scholarships retained their student status: the sample included one member of an interdisciplinary doctoral training school. Although, as is usually the case for this kind of position, the interviewee did not have any teaching assignments, she was still teaching one or two courses. Other interview participants had the status of employees. The majority were scientific assistants (*Wissenschaftliche MitarbeiterInnen*) with full- or part-time (half) positions involved in research and with a diverse teaching load. A lecturer for special assignments (*Lehrkraft für besondere Aufgaben*) is a position only in teaching in which the teaching load can be very high. It was up to 13 academic hours per week in the case of one informant. Associate lecturer (*Lehrbeauftragte*) is a position only in teaching and usually for one term, aimed at covering the specific teaching demand; these interviewees were teaching one or two courses. The employment contracts for the positions mentioned are usually for up to 2 years; the contracts for associate lectures, for one term. An assistant lecturer with a short-term contract (*Akademischer Rat (auf Zeit)*) who participated in the research had both teaching and research assignments with a higher remuneration than that of a scientific assistant; his contract was for 4 years. Nonetheless, such salary differences are not found in every case; the position of *Akademischer Rat* gives a status of civil servant with or without tenure, and a scientific assistant is an employee.

The selection was made to ensure diversity in the sample in terms of gender, employment situation, work assignments, organizational context, as well as the representation of different disciplines in the social sciences. The disciplinary focus was to ensure homogeneity in academic work characteristics in terms of not only teaching and research but also the job opportunities in the labour market outside academia.

Coding used the procedures of Grounded Theory (Strauss/Corbin 1998). The specific thematic focus was on teaching in the context of other professional activities. Additional inspiration for coding was the research literature on less prestigious types of work within the symbolic interactionist methodological framework in which the work content has been related to different societal discourses and individual justification strategies (Meisenbach 2008).

4 Results

I shall concentrate my analysis on one interviewee, Maria. Maria is an especially interesting case, because she was involved in different kinds of teaching and research at the university. The consequences of the structures of the academic labour market in the narrower scope of the university with regard to how teaching and research are framed and with regard to decision making become very noticeable in the interview.

Maria has a full-time position as a scientific assistant with a teaching load of four academic hours per week. Parallel to that, she is working on her doctoral thesis. In the past, she had taken vocational training and worked in public education services outside the university.

She is teaching large student groups on the bachelor level, but also has experience of teaching small groups of master students. She is qualifying as a researcher, that is, works on her own research project in the form of writing a dissertation. At the same time, she is involved in a working group: an externally financed research project at the university.

4.1 Teaching

Framings of Maria's teaching are rather specific, particular, and very much bounded to the context of the university. The way she frames teaching is related to the characteristics of teaching she is currently practising. Maria is teaching compulsory courses (*Pflichtseminare*), and it is difficult for her to relate her teaching to the topic of her research. Maria stresses that she spends almost half of her working time on teaching, including holding seminars, reviewing student papers, replying to their emails, and advising them.

The material reality of her teaching she refers to is the bachelor level teaching: standardized content not related to her research interests, large student groups, and diverse students in terms of their motivation and background knowledge.

Maria notes that she lowered her demands on students and on herself as a teacher when she switched from teaching seminars on the master level to the bachelor level. She noticed that students "do not manage in the seminar". As a consequence, she says she is less enthusiastic about teaching, more careless, and allocates less time to preparation:

> I don't prepare for the seminars that much anymore. ...to the situation that students don't manage in the seminar, I tell myself: "it is indeed not a problem" ... and of course I am a bit less enthusiastic when I stand in front of the students. (Maria)

She continues discussing her teaching with reference to the material reality of teaching on the bachelor level. Students have different capacities and not all of them manage well in the seminar. That is why she faces a problem in how to deal with this.

She tries to overcome the problem by relying on the importance of study goals and relocates her autonomy over deciding on her ways of teaching to the general goals of the studies and the relevance of her teaching for the future professional practice of the students. Despite the fact that students may have different background knowledge and motivations, the teacher should have an

> understanding of what the students actually have to learn in their studies, and that you do not say, 'well, they are not that advanced in their studies yet', or 'they don't want this', but that you keep your own profile in the seminar. (Maria)

This framing of teaching is very university-contextualized and it stresses study goals and points indirectly to the importance of the study programme. That means that she as a teacher would like to be goal-oriented and put frames on her way of teaching. Setting goals is an important procedure to relate the seminar to the overall study experience of the students at the university in a strategic way. The particular technique she relies on is to stick to the "profile", so the goals of the studies are in balance with the goals of the teacher. In this way, "good teaching" can be ensured.

In relation to this, she stresses that teaching has to be relevant for the future work of the students, to address the problems their professional practice:

> Good teaching... is about how the problems considered in the seminar come up in practice and how one could possibly react to them. (Maria)

This framing of teaching is of a particular character: it stresses teaching being outcome-oriented, clearly structured, and not changing arbitrarily. Further framings of teaching can be considered as particular, referring to particular aspects of teaching, such as "teaching as seminar talk production".

The framing of producing communication in the seminar can be seen as being both very technical and, at the same time, very university-specific due to the reference to students who are difficult to deal with:

> A good seminar is when the students talk and communicate with each other, with me, that is, there is a productive atmosphere, and that there it is only talked, but then it is exactly ... the production of the seminar talk. (Maria)

The situation when students do not talk in the seminar is a sign of bad teaching (Maria: 65). That is why it is generally important that students "react and actively participate" (Maria: 69).

4.2 Research

When framing research, Maria stresses particular and more applied aspects of it, rather than the aspects related to dealing with abstract knowledge. "Scientific" (*wissenschaftliche*) work, that is academic work, can take the form of "preparing presentations", "writing articles", or "sitting concentrated on the dissertation" (Maria).

When it comes to the activities she engages in as a scientist, she talks about her research work in the team:

> We developed questionnaires, organized a survey. Then we had to write reports, make presentations of our results ... (Maria).

She stresses the benefits of working in a team: one can gain support and share responsibility for success. She gives an example of making a presentation to the clients. The latter are associated with the non-academic environment that is alienated and hostile.

4.3 Teaching and research relation

Maria's framings of academic work including teaching and research are of a particular character; that is, they refer to particular techniques and procedures rather than the abstract idea of scientific knowledge processing. In addition, these framings are very much contextualized. That means they refer to either university structures of teaching such as the curriculum or study programme or to characteristics of the students. Or they refer to the context of research in a working group, including work sharing, workload distribution, and confidence in her work derived from group membership. The interview data shows the persistence of the idea of the unity of teaching and research as soon as the interviewee refers to both when narrating on different components of her work. Thus, it is interesting to see how Maria relates both spheres of academic work: teaching and research.

The narrations on the material reality of teaching including the high teaching load and standardized teaching unrelated to the topic of research emerge together with more specific and context-bounded framings of teaching. On the one hand, academic work is "that one prepares presentations, writes articles" (Maria), and good teaching is rather about bringing in new things and being up to date. This leads to the way of reformulating the teaching and research relation for her situation. This situation includes a relatively high teaching load, responsibilities in the research project, and lack of time for her own research project – her dissertation. Importantly, positions below professorship are generally considered as a qualification stage on the way to becoming a scientist in Germany. During this stage, carrying out independent research, that is writing a dissertation, is pivotal.

She relies on the framing that being up to date is what makes her teaching good and makes it into university teaching. If structural changes increase the workload, this major prerequisite of university teaching might be lost. She makes a remark regarding university positions with a very high teaching load:

For instance, the posts with eighteen hours of teaching per week, that makes 9 seminars per week, they are, I think, difficult to do, because then you really want to bring in new things and to be at the forefront of the scientific debate, then you can become like a teacher at school, that is, and there it is then easier. There you probably do not have to be at the forefront of the scientific debate. (Maria)

At the same time, such conditions of high workload legitimize teaching being less related to the "scientific debate", or to research. She relies on the framings of university teaching as based on "being up to date", "informed". These aspects of teaching are seen by the informant as the major difference between school teaching and university teaching. When the structures are changing, it is legitimate to weaken the interrelation between teaching and research. In the case of a high teaching load, one does not have to be necessarily at the forefront of the scientific debate.

The contextualized framing of teaching is related to the discourse on "the students difficult to deal with". The students are difficult to deal with because of their diversity and growing numbers. The framing justifies changes in teaching as work, but teaching is still bounded to the specific context of the university in the implicit reference to students and study goals.

The agency analysis focuses on whether the framings of teaching and research are non-contradictory for this interviewee. Her framing of teaching is in balance with the framing of research. The linkage between teaching and research is reformulated into the relation between the activities that are considered in rather technical and specific terms: as reading and "being up to date".

Research for her is also reading, that is why, by doing teaching, when she has to read a lot, she is approaching research work, and it can be supposed that her framing of "research as also reading" approaches the conceptualization of research as a rather theoretical research. This, in turn, implies that theoretical research is also reading:

Well, research for me is the most exciting activity among all in academic work. I think teaching is also very important, and I also don't think that teaching and research must be always coupled with each other; that is, you can also do good teaching when you are not doing research yourself. I am convinced of that, in that that, particularly, if you have a very narrow definition of research. That is, you are doing research, yes, you are researching, yes, also by approaching closer the subject theoretically. That is, when you read a lot, I think you can do very good teaching too without doing own research projects. (Maria)

The citation below illustrates that she would like to claim that reading is an important aspect of good teaching. The relation between teaching and research is established through this activity:

Although sometimes I have even a feeling, particularly, when I am preparing now for my seminars, I still read for example also a lot. (Maria)

Thus, teaching, research, and the relation between those two components of academic work is framed in this interview in a particular way. In addition, it is very much university-contextualized. In relation to this, it can be asked how she relates her work to her professional future in a meaningful way. When analysing this, the interview reveals a conflict.

Maria gives an account that shows how decision making and thus action is blocked as a result of a conflict in professional orientations:

Particularly, this is very difficult in a life of a scientist. Exactly when you want this, that is, when you would like to stay at the university, within the regulation six plus six years,[1] and

---

1 *Wissenschaftszeitvertragsgesetz*, according to which employment in positions funded from the university budget is limited in time up to 12 years (6 years before obtaining doctoral degree and 6 after).

now it is not the case for me that I have a clear goal, that I <u>necessarily</u> want to become a professor, and at the moment I am thinking it over. Where can it lead to? Should it be teaching indeed for me? I think there are already many committed people who can take the lecturer positions ... working in projects ... what would be a very insecure perspective of course, because I have now to work 30 years more before retirement, that would be quite a few projects (laughing), which you should have been doing, if you take into account that the long projects themselves well, normally, don't last longer than for 3 years. Or then again possibly to have to reorient outside of academia, either to some research institutes, consultancy institutes, or think it over again in a completely different way. It is a very strange situation because I learned a profession before, and then was thinking ok, now I'll go to the university and learn something different once again, but then I have my profession and I am continuing practising it and now one is in the life of a scientist and actually it is even more precarious. (Maria)

Research as a component of academic work is related to the discourse of "living a life of a scientist". "A life of a scientist" is about "emotional pressures that the life of a scientist brings, that you question yourself, that you get angry, that you sometimes exaggerate in one direction or another, that you do not let up" (Maria). It is also about a blurred boundary between private life and working life and about working overtime: "well, we all here at the university work actually more, because it is enjoyable" (Maria).

She relies on this discourse to justify the lack of infrastructure for professional development for her in academia, as she says, beyond becoming a researcher, that is getting a professorship.

The rather organizationally contextualized and "particular" framing of research would not be in balance with the idea that such research can be an overwhelming activity that would absorb the life of an individual as whole and be related to some difficulties to cope with such as unstable employment, risks in career development, challenges to balance work and life, and so forth.

The particular framings of academic work do not fit the existing professional discourses on what it means to be a researcher and available career development structures. Moreover, the framing of "living a life of a scientist" justifies a lack of sufficient professional development opportunities and keeps her from making a decision about her career. The tension between different professional orientations and structural conditions characterize this conflict.

In the case of this interview, the framings of teaching and research support each other, that is, they act as symbolic resources in framing academic work. This illustrates that although self-reflexivity is enabled, the professional discourses and the material reality of the teaching load and the lack of career development structures apart from professorship do not support agency in the dimension of resources. The opposite is the case: contradictions arise.

On the one hand, the professional discourse of "living a life of a scientist" is important in the case of this informant in explaining the challenging reality of her employment at the university: the inability to plan and being exposed to short-term contracts. This employment situation is seen as being related to the specificity of the profession, qualifying into a researcher. On the other hand, the ideal of being a scientist contradicts with her conceptualization of research, which is of a particular character – furthermore, with the material reality of her work in which she does not have enough time left to concentrate on her qualification to be a researcher – her dissertation.

In other words, the discourse of "living the life of a scientist" can be emancipatory, that is, resourceful, when she addresses the lack of resources for career development in the material reality of her work. At the same time, this discourse is in conflict with her framing of research and teaching; this contradiction blocks decision making and also agency when she narrates on her future development: she postpones the decision. The re-orientation towards contexts "outside" academia is blocked, because it questions her previous decisions and requires "completely different ways of thinking". This means that there is a lack of resources for recontextualization. "Living a life of a scientist" is a professional discourse and constitutes a structure that incorporates the "boundary making" on both symbolic and material levels.[2]

For that reason, it is possible to speak about adjustment, rather than development here,[3] especially in the case of the structure of "living a life of a scientist" on which the informant relies. This structure constrains agency. The institutional framework of the academic labour market does not support her framing of teaching and research in the narrower context of university employment and career. Many researchers have pointed to the insecure situation of scientific assistants and increasing completion for permanent positions, such as professorships (e.g. Klecha/Reimer 2008; Gülker 2010, Lange-Vester/Teiwes-Kügler 2013).

5 Conclusions and discussion

Self-reflexivity or reasoned action is characteristic of "skilful actors" (see Fligstein 2001); that is those actors who challenge the existing structures. In other words, agency is characteristic of those actors who can overcome them by reframing and recontextualizing themselves and their work.

In the case of Maria, her framing of research and teaching were particular, university-contextualized, and in balance with each other. It was possible to

---

2   Such as "being too old to working in business"; "there outside, they speak a different language"; etc. – examples from other interviews, in case of this interview - the perceived "hostility" or "another way of thinking outside" blocks cooperation possibilities in the broader context of the academic labour market.
3   The concept of adaptive preferences of the CA might be relevant for characterizing it (see e.g. Quizilbash 2007).

establish the relation between teaching and research through the idea of being up to date in the scientific debate and reading. It makes her current work as a teacher on the Bachelor level and as a researcher in an externally funded project at the university justifiable and meaningful. This framing corresponds with the idea to formulate and promote research-based teaching (Huber et al. 2009).

However, her work situation does not allow her to spend enough time on her dissertation and this does not match well with the professional discourse of living a life of a scientist and qualifying as a researcher. This discourse is nonetheless important. She relies on it to justify her lack of career development opportunities in the sense of getting a permanent university position in the future. As a result, the conflict in professional development orientations is not resolved; it does not allow her to meaningfully relate her current work to a professional future. Postponing decisions regarding possible career transitions indicates that her action is blocked. At the same time, the coexistence of different discourses and framings that are in a contention indicates that the way academics see their work changes, and that there is a dynamic in the meanings of its components.

From the perspective of the evaluation of professional development in the dimension of agency, greater self-reflection is the case for this informant when she sees teaching as activities of a particular character. Her framings of teaching are nonetheless placed in the university context. However, there is a lack of support for this framing in the resources aspect. The reasons for this are, on the one hand, the academic labour market structures including the professional discourse of being a scientist; on the other hand, the lack of present structural possibilities of stable employment in the university or the problems with a transition to the labour market outside the university.

Research shows that when designing personnel development policies and respective organizational structures, it is important to consider the aspects related to material reality and symbolic aspects of the work of academics. These include contract lengths, the availability of stable positions, the number of teaching- or research-intensive positions, career development structures, and the framings of academic work – particularly teaching. The policies developed based on ascribing research-like characteristics to teaching without providing stable employment conditions and without reward and promotion criteria to encourage teaching are open to criticism. The policies supporting agency should not mean just a relocation of risks and responsibilities to the actors, but efforts to ensure their abilities to choose and be flexible in seeking new opportunities both inside and outside academia. Different types of teaching and teachers have to be taken into account when developing academic staff at universities. The interview extracts presented in the chapter showed that, on one hand, the professional discourses on research sometimes constrain agency. Some regulations such as *Wissenschaftszeitvertragsgesetz*, as well as a lack of stable jobs apart from professorship do not support a recontextualization of the framings of academic work. These framings were formulated in a more particular way in the context of the actual teaching and research practice. An important way to enhance agency and development would be to improve the material reality of teaching, so that it would allow young academics to spend more time on their own dissertations and provide them with stable employment and professional growth opportunities.

References

Alkire, Sabina. (2002): Valuing Freedoms: Sen's Capability Approach and Poverty Reduction., Oxford: Oxford University Press.
Ash, Mitchell G (2006): Bachelor of What, Master of Whom? The Humboldt Myth and Historical Transformations of Higher Education in German-Speaking Europe and the US. In: European Journal of Education, 41, 2, pp. 245–267.
Bloch Roland/Burkhardt, Anke/Franz, Anja/Kieslich, Claudia/Kreckel, Reiner/Schuster, Robert/Trümpler, Doreen/Schulze, Henning/Zimmermann, Karin (2011): Personalreform zwischen föderaler Möglichkeit und institutioneller Wirklichkeit. In: Pasternack, Peer (ed.): Hochschulen nach der Föderalismusreform, Leipzig: Akademische Verlagsanstalt, pp. 155–214.
Comim, Flavio (2001): Operationalizing Sen's Capability Approach. Paper prepared at the Conference Justice and Poverty: Examining Sen's Capability Approach, Cambridge (unpubl.).
Cummings, William K./Shin, Jung. C (2013): Teaching and Research in Contemporary Higher Education: An Overview. In: Shin, Jung Cheol/Arimoto, Akira/Cummings, William K./Teichler, Ulrich (eds.): Teaching and Research in Contemporary Higher Education. Systems, Activities and Rewards. Dordrecht: Springer Netherlands, pp. 1–14.
Emirbayer, Mustafa (1997): Manifesto for a Relational Sociology. In: American Journal of Sociology, 103, 2, pp. 281–317.
Fligstein, Neil (2001): Social Skill and the Theory of Fields. In: Sociological Theory, 19, 2, pp. 105–125.
Giddens, Anthony (1984): The Constitution of Society. Berkley: University of California Press.
Gülker, Silke. (2010): Autonomer, aber weiter unsicher. Neue Führungspositionen haben das Karrieresystem in der deutschen Wissenschaft nur wenig verändert. WZBrief Arbeit. Berlin: WZB.
Henkel, Mary (2000): Academic Identities and Policy Change in Higher Education. London, Philadelphia: Jessica Kingsley.
Huber, Ludwig/Hellmer, Julia/Schneider, Friederike (eds.) (2009): Forschendes Lernen im Studium. Aktuelle Konzepte und Erfahrungen. Bielefeld: UVW.
Kehm, Barbara M. (2012): The Academics and the Higher Education Professionals. Paper presented at the conference "Changing Conditions and Changing Approaches of Academic Work", June 4–6, Berlin (unpubl.).

Klecha, Stefan/Reimer, Melanie (2008): Wissenschaft als besonderer Arbeitsmarkt, Grundtypologien des Umgangs mit unsicherer Beschäftigung beim wissenschaftlichen Personal. In: Klecha, Stefan/Krumbein, Wolfgang (eds.): Die Beschäftigungssituation von wissenschaftlichem Nachwuchs. Wiesbaden: VS Verlag, pp. 13–87.

Krais, Beate (2008): Wissenschaft als Lebensform: Die alltagspraktische Seite akademischer Karrieren. In: Haffner, Yvonne/Krais, Beate (eds.): Arbeit als Lebensform? Berufliche Erfolg, private Lebensführung und Chancengleichheit in akademischen Berufsfeldern, Frankfurt/M.: Campus, pp. 177–211.

Krücken, Georg/Kosmützky, Anna/Torka, Marc (eds.) (2007): Towards a Multiversity? Universities between Global Trends and National Traditions. Science Studies. Bielefeld: transcript.

Krücken, Georg (2003): Learning the New 'New Thing'. On the Role of Path Dependency in University Structures. In: Higher Education, 42, pp. 315–339.

Lange-Vester, Andrea/Teiwes-Kügler, Christel (2013): Zwischen W3 und Hartz IV. Arbeistsituation und Perspektiven wissenschaftlicher Mitarbeiterinnen und Mitarbeiter. Opladen: Verlag Barbara Budrich.

Meisenbach, Rebecca J. (2008): Working With Tensions: Materiality, Discourse, and (Dis)empowerment in Occupational Identity Negotiation Among Higher Education Fund-Raisers. In: Management Communication Quarterly, 22, 2, pp. 258–287.

Musselin, Christine (2007): The Transformation of Academic Work: Facts and Analysis. Working paper CSHE, 4.07. Retrieved from http://escholarship.org/uc/item/5c10883g#page-1

Musselin, Christine (2011): The Academic Workplace. What we already know, what we still do not know, what we would like to know. In: Rhoten, Diana/Calhoun, Craig. (eds.): Knowledge Matters. The Public Mission of the Research University. New York: Columbia University Press – SSRC Book, pp. 423–457.

Quizilbash, Muzzafair (2007): Social Choice and Individual Capabilities. In: Politics Philosophy Economics, 6, 2, pp. 169–192.

Sen, Amartya (1999): Development as Freedom. Oxford: Oxford University Press.

Shin, Hae-Ran (2011): Spatial capability for understanding gendered mobility for Korean Christian immigrant women in Los Angeles. In: Urban Studies, 48, pp. 2355–2373.

Strauss, Anselm. L./Corbin, Juliett (1998): Basics of Qualitative Research: Techniques and Procedures for Developing Grounded Theory. 2nd ed. Newbury Park, CA: Sage.

Teichler, Ulrich (2013): Teaching and Research in Germany: The Notions of University Professors. In: Shin, Jung Cheol/Arimoto, Akira/Cummings, William K./Teichler, Ulrich (eds.): Teaching and Research in Contemporary Higher Education. Systems, Activities and Rewards. Dordrecht: Springer Netherlands, pp. 61–88.

Witzel, Andreas (1985): Das problemzentrierte Interview. In: Jüttemann, Gerd (ed.): Qualitative Forschung in der Psychologie. Grundfragen, Verfahrensweisen, Anwendungsfelder. Weinheim, Basel: Beltz, pp. 227–256.

Index

Adaptive preferences 9, 117, 170
Agency 8, 12, 19f., 24ff., 29, 33, 36, 76ff., 83, 94, 115ff., 126, 131, 135ff., 145f., 149, 153ff., 160ff., 168ff.
Aspiration 78, 83, 131
Biographical research 12, 141, 143, 145f., 148f., 154
Capability constraints 106, 125f., 132, 134ff.
Capability set 34ff., 45, 47, 154
Childhood studies 12, 126, 136, 138
Choice 9, 19, 27, 30, 34ff., 39, 47, 63, 68, 75, 78, 116, 119f., 127, 133, 142, 144
Conversion factor 10f., 19f., 27, 30, 36f., 40, 45, 76, 117, 119, 149
Critical discourse analysis 33ff.
Critical materialist theory 11, 53ff.
Education policy 11, 33ff., 40, 45ff., 66, 73f., 80, 83f., 89, 159
Education system 7, 11, 42f., 50, 53, 74, 77f., 80f., 83, 85f., 96, 100, 105, 117
Educational politics 11, 53, 55ff., 60f., 63, 65ff.
Ethnographic research 11, 107, 109, 112, 118f.
Family 7, 29, 45, 53f., 63, 69, 81, 84, 112f., 115, 118f., 132ff., 141ff., 149ff., 153
Freedom 8f., 11f., 21, 30ff., 34, 39f., 47, 50, 59, 70, 76, 78, 83, 85, 94, 110, 115f., 133, 144ff., 149, 151ff., 160
Functionings 8f., 12, 19f., 27, 30, 35ff., 39f., 42, 76, 83, 85f., 92, 94, 107, 114ff., 147, 154
Higher education 78, 107, 156
Human capital 55f., 61, 73ff., 80, 83, 85f., 114, 117

Intersectionality 107f., 110, 112, 115ff., 130
Justice 7ff., 12, 21, 30, 34, 54f., 64, 67f., 73, 77, 83f., 86, 126, 128ff.
L'homme capable 10, 21ff.
Labour market 7, 12, 54, 144, 150f., 153f., 159, 161, 164, 170f.
O-capabilities 38, 78
Opportunity freedom 12, 144, 149, 154
Policy analysis 11, 33ff., 40f., 43f., 47
Preferences 9, 39, 64ff., 117, 150, 160, 170
Pre-school 7, 89, 93f., 95f., 99, 101, 106
Primary school 11, 17, 19, 24, 29, 77ff., 89, 91, 102, 151
Rights 38, 43f., 73, 76, 125ff., 135, 138f.
S-capabilities 38, 78
School system 54, 56, 58, 63
Secondary school 56, 79f., 96
Social context 8ff., 34ff., 114, 154, 161
Social justice 7ff., 12, 34, 54, 67, 73, 83, 86, 129f.
Social policy 10, 84, 143f., 154
Structural equation model 97
University 12, 42, 159, 161, 163ff.
Vocational training 57, 143, 150ff., 164
Welfare 12, 37, 53f., 61, 125, 141ff., 151ff.
Well-being 7, 20, 25f., 29f., 32, 34f., 39, 44, 47f., 50, 55f., 67f., 76ff., 83f., 86, 119, 144, 151
Youth 12, 53f., 57ff., 66f., 116, 144, 147, 149, 152ff.

Social Work & Public Policy

HANS-UWE OTTO & ANDREAS POLUTTA & HOLGER ZIEGLER (EDS.)
Evidence-based Practice – Modernising the Knowledge Base of Social Work?
2009. 254 pp. Pb. 26,00 € (D), US$ 39.95, GBP 22.95
ISBN 978-3-86649-121-2
Written for students and practitioners of social work and social policy, this volume features selected writings on evidence-based practices and how these new perspectives re-evaluate and reshape "the character of welfare professionalism".
Reference & Research Book News August 2009

This book undoubtedly provides a forum for moving the debate about evidence-based practice beyond the simplistic for-against arguments towards a meaningful exploration of future directions for social work.
Voluntas: International Journal of Voluntary and Nonprofit Organizations
23.01.2010

HANS-UWE OTTO & HOLGER ZIEGLER (EDS.)
Education, Welfare and the Capabilities Approach
A European Perspective
2010. 240 pp. 29,90 € (D), US$ 45.95, GBP 26.95
ISBN 978-3-86649-290-5
The authors assess the potentials and pitfalls of the Capabilities Approach to issues of education and welfare. Renowned philosophers, sociologists, psychologists, economists and educational scientists explore the conceptual and practical implications of this approach for delivering socially just policies.

Verlag Barbara Budrich • Barbara Budrich Publishers
Stauffenbergstr. 7. D-51379 Leverkusen Opladen
Tel +49 (0)2171.344.594 • Fax +49 (0)2171.344.693 • info@budrich-verlag.de

www.barbara-budrich.net